Date Due

Implementing Capital Budgeting Techniques

THE FINANCIAL MANAGEMENT ASSOCIATION SURVEY AND SYNTHESIS SERIES

This unique series provides corporate executives and professional investors with the practical tools vital for making sound financial decisions in today's competitive markets. Comprehensive and readable, each book in the series focuses on a relevant topic, integrating research with the day-to-day concerns of finance practitioners. Other books in this continuing series are:

The FMA Series is part of the larger Institutional Investor Series in Finance.

The costs of research and development that made the Financial Management Association Survey and Synthesis Series possible were underwritten in part by support provided to the Financial Management Association by United Airlines, the Federal Reserve Bank of Philadelphia, and Ameritech.

IMPLEMENTING CAPITAL BUDGETING TECHNIQUES

Revised Edition

Harold Bierman, Jr.

BALLINGER PUBLISHING COMPANY
Cambridge, Massachusetts
A Subsidiary of Harper & Row, Publishers, Inc.

International Standard Book Number: 0-88730-359-5

Library of Congress Catalog Card Number: 88-19404

Printed in the United States of America

Library of Congress

Bierman, Harold.

Implementing capital budgeting techniques / Harold Bierman, Jr. — Rev. ed.

p.   cm. — (Institutional investor series in finance) (The Financial Management Association survey and synthesis series)
Rev. ed. of: Implementation of capital budgeting techniques. c1986.
Includes index.
ISBN 0-88730-359-5
1. Capital budget.   2. Capital investments.   I. Bierman, Harold. Implementation of capital budgeting techniques.   II. Title.   III. Title: Capital budgeting techniques.   IV. Series.   V. Series: The Financial Management Association survey and synthesis series.

HG4028.C4B544   1988   88-19404
658.1'54—dc19   CIP

Contents

Preface

In 1951 two books opened the door to new managerial techniques for making capital budgeting decisions: discounted cash flow methods of evaluating investments. *Capital Budgeting* was written by Joel Dean, and *The Theory of Investment of the Firm* by Vera and Friedrich Lutz.

Dean, a respected academician who did a large amount of consulting, wrote his book for business managers. The Lutzes, as economists interested in capital theory, wrote theirs for their professional colleagues. Both books were extremely well written and understandable. They made both academics and business managers start to think about how investments should be evaluated.

Over thirty years have elapsed since the beginning of this capital budgeting revolution. The objective of this book is to review the state of the art today, with a particular emphasis on what managers perceive to be problems in implementing capital budgeting techniques.

We surveyed 257 financial officers of the largest Fortune 500 industrial firms requesting them to identify problems of implementation. The 102 replies received form the motivation for the topics discussed in this book. A collective thank you is offered to all the busy executives who took the time to write thoughtful letters concerning their capital budgeting decisions. Excerpts from their letters appear in the Appendix.

This book describes perceived problems of implementation, surveys the capital budgeting literature dealing with these problems, and suggests ways of coping with them. It is an attempt to link the academic capital budgeting literature with the current interests of business managers. If this book is successful the reader will be able to implement known capital budgeting techniques with somewhat more confidence and usefulness, and equally important, will understand the limits of our knowledge concerning capital budgeting.

In writing this book, I have greatly benefited from review of the manuscript by Richard S. Bower, Ronald C. Lease, Rodney L. Roenfeldt, and Robert A. Taggart.

Harold Bierman, Jr.
Cornell University

Implementing Capital Budgeting Techniques

1

What We Know about
Capital Budgeting

But, I would much rather bet on instinct than a
random DCF model.
A Vice President, Finance

There are two extreme stands regarding capital budgeting that are definitely wrong. One is that the conventional discounted cash flow calculations are a waste of time or worse, because they are based on uncertain cash flows. The use of discounted cash flow calculations offer only an illusion of exactness that affords a false sense of security to the decisionmaker. The second wrong position is that discounted cash flow calculations always provide exact reliable answers to complex problems and that no further analysis or judgment is necessary to make a decision. Both of these positions are faulty.

This chapter reviews what is known and accepted about capital budgeting decisions. It is important to understand the problems management can solve before proceeding to problems that management cannot solve exactly.

Even today, major corporations are failing to use the knowledge about capital budgeting that is universally accepted by academics. Consider the chairman of the board (and chief operations officer) of one of Fortune's 100 who ignores the net present value measure and regularly requests and uses a return-on-asset measure that values a dollar received in year ten as much as a dollar received today. This type of error in decisionmaking technique is unnecessary.

Some corporations do not think they have problems with capital budgeting decisions. For example, one executive of a Fortune 500 firm in a capital-intensive industry stated: "[This company] has not experienced any significant difficulties in implementing its capital budgeting techniques." It is very unlikely that any corporation does not have problems implementing conventional capital budgeting techniques. Problems inevitably accompany uncertainty.

The problem of obtaining reliable inputs for the calculations often is cited as a reason for not using sophisticated capital budgeting techniques (such as net present value). For example, a classic observation of universal importance was made by one executive: "The real challenge is creativity and invention, not analysis. Timely execution of projects by entrepreneurial managers is also more critical than sophistication of analytical budgeting techniques."

An academic must respond: Is it not possible to combine creativity, invention, and good analytical capital budgeting techniques? The choice is not a matter of "either/or." Rather, managers must use the best tools available. Consider the case of an oil company evaluating two drastically different methods of converting heavy oil to usuable products. The difference in investment is $3 billion; there also are differences in benefits. The information on which the decision is to be made is very reliable. In such circumstances there is one basic theoretically correct way of evaluating the two alternatives—and many incorrect ways. Given the current state of knowledge, it is wasteful to make this decision incorrectly.

The 1984–1985 Survey of Finance Officers

For this survey I sent letters to 257 senior financial officers of the largest Fortune 500 firms. Seventeen letters were returned unopened, so effectively no more than 240 letters were sent. Twelve respondents could not participate (two of the firms had been acquired), so there were no more than 228 possible participants. Replies were received from 102 firms, so that the response rate was 102/228 = 45 percent. (Including the firms that chose not to participate, the response rate was 114/240 = 48 percent.)

The survey letter read: "I would greatly appreciate a letter from you describing one or more difficulties that your firm has had in implementing capital budgeting techniques. Your comments can be brief or long. Any observations would be of assistance. I need information relative to the types of difficulties you have encountered."

As there was no attempt to structure the request for information, the managers supplied a wide range of thoughts on capital budgeting that turned out to be very revealing (See Appendix). The first request letter was sent in November 1984; a follow-up letter was sent to nonrespondents in March 1985. Table 1–1 summarizes the information collected.

Table 1–1. Difficulties in Implementing Capital Budgeting Techniques
Results of 1984–1985 Survey (102 Responses of 228 Effective Requests)

Problem Described	Number of Firms Identifying Problem[a]
Strategy considerations	27
Risk Analysis	27
Capital rationing	16
Difficulty of auditing results	15
Hurdle rate determination	15 .
Communications, selling the system, and education	10
An inability to quantify	10
Accounting versus investment criteria	9
Cash flow–risk considerations	9
Structure and organization for evaluation of investments	8
Cash flow–mechanics of calculation	8

a. Some firms listed more than one problem of implementation, and some reported no problems.

If we recognize that strategy problems arise because of risk, the survey results indicate that risk (uncertainty) is by far the major problem faced. Six firms also mentioned excessive optimism, a form of risk, and twelve firms said they had problems with determining the amount and timing of capital expenditures (another form of risk). While it was expressed in a variety of ways, the challenge of incorporating risk considerations is by far the number one problem seen in capital budgeting decisions.

The responses revealed two things about the choice of the method of evaluating investments. First, some managers are still confused as to the relative merits of the net present value and internal rate of return methods, as well as not cognizant of the limitations of return on investment (ROI). Second, the choice of method is considered to be a minor problem compared to the other difficulties of implementing investment decisions.

Among the interesting issues that were mentioned by one or more firms, but not frequently enough to be included in the table, are

◆ Excessive red tape
◆ Resistance to change
◆ Inflation (this tended to be raised by firms with large foreign operations)
◆ Choice of tax rates
◆ Forecasting exchange rates
◆ Excessive optimism

In 1985 firms were much more concerned about trying to cope with the problems of determining the choice of industry in which the investments are to be made (strategy), and with reasonable unbiased forecasts of the future, than they are with refining their methods of evaluation.

Review of the Literature and Practice

A Brief Historical Review

Modern capital budgeting can be said to have begun with the early writings of Irving Fisher, yet there was a twenty-year wait for the next step.[1] In 1951 two books written by economists introduced the concept of the internal rate of return for measuring the expected profitability of an investment. Joel Dean's *Captial Budgeting*[2] written for a business audience, is characterized by total lack of reference to any previous academic literature. The second book, *The Theory of Investment of the Firm*, was written by Friedrich and Vera Lutz.[3] The second chapter of the Lutzs's book summarizes alternative methods of evaluating investments, as well as the economic antecedents of applied capital budgeting techniques.

Before publication of these two books, managers tended to use methods such as payback or average income divided by average investment to evaluate investments. Such methods fail to consider the time value of money. These two pathfinding books (which today are still useful reading) immediately caused people to start thinking about how investment decisions should be made so that the time value of money is considered, and a flood of papers and articles followed shortly.

A 1954 article in the *Harvard Business Review* by Dean was particularly important in introducing business managers to a discounted cash flow approach to capital budgeting.[4] Dean recommended the use of a rate-of-return method, which consisted of finding a percentage (the rate of discount) that caused the sum of the present values of the cash flows to be equal to zero. This was a relatively easily understood measure, as it described the profitability of an investment in terms that were analogous to the yield of a bond. The internal rate of return was intuitively appealing to practical business managers, for it was easily understood.

As the internal rate of return technique rapidly became accepted by a wide range of industrial firms (with chemical and oil firms leading the way), there was some confusion about the relative merits of the internal rate of return (a percentage) method and the net present value (a dollar amount) method. A famous issue of the University of Chicago's *Journal of Business* in October 1955 described the confusion that existed. It included a classic paper by Lorie and Savage that summarized difficulties in using the internal rate of return method to evaluate mutually exclusive investments.[5] (Many of these *Journal of Business* papers were reproduced in Solomon's 1959 readings book dealing with the management of corporate capital.[6])

The confusion as to the relative merits of net present value and internal rate of return persisted in the theoretical literature until 1958 when Jack Hirshleifer published a paper in the *Journal of Political Economy* that drew heavily on the classic book by Irving Fisher, *The Theory of Interest*.[7] In this paper, Hirshleifer laid out the theoretical foundation for understanding the similarities and differences between the net present value and internal rate of return methods of making capital budgeting decisions.

In 1960 Seymour Smidt and I published *The Capital Budgeting Decision*.[8] This book applied the academic literature to a wide range of business problems and helped supply a needed link between the academic and the business communities. The seventh editor was published in 1988.

Literature published since 1951 has had an impressive impact on the capital budgeting decisionmaking techniques of corporations throughout the world. Numerous surveys of corporate investment practices highlight the extensive changes that have taken place.

Changing Capital Budgeting Methods: Surveys 1955–1983

In 1966 the Stanford Research Institute published the results of a 1965 survey of Fortune 500 firms conducted by Robichek and McDonald.[9] Of the 163 corporations responding, 47 percent used at least one discounted cash flow method. The same survey revealed that in 1955 only 9 percent of these firms had used a discounted cash flow method. From the birth of modern capital budgeting literature in 1951 to the year 1965 we see a widespread adoption of discounted cash flow techniques by the largest firms in U.S. industry. Later surveys show that the dispersion of understanding continued at a rapid pace into the 1980s.

Schall, Sundem, and Geijsbeek published a 1978 paper based on 189 responses to a survey questionnaire sent to 424 large U.S. corporations.[10] They found that 86 percent of the firms responding used either internal rate of return or net present value (both discounted cash flow techniques).

Extrapolating from the observations of these surveys, we can conclude that nearly all the finance departments of the largest firms were using one or more discounted cash flow method for evaluating investment alternatives by 1985. But these surveys reveal nothing about how nonfinance officers or small corporations make investment decisions. Also, we should not conclude that use of discounted cash flow means investment decisions are being made in a reasonable manner. It is possible to use any discounted cash flow method in a manner that will negate its usefulness.

Besides the two surveys of the capital budgeting practices of large firms, there are many other surveys of interest. Numerous survey papers were published between 1961 and 1984.[11-26] The most important conclusion we can draw from the surveys is that business practice relative to capital budgeting decisions has improved tremendously in the past thirty years. Few of the largest firms are not familiar with the discounted cash flow techniques.

Alternative Methods of Evaluating Investments

Accepting that discounted cash flow methods are widely used, we can review four methods, focusing on the assumptions than form the basis of these approaches. There are more methods of capital budgeting used by business firms than the four methods to be described here, but just about all reasonable alternatives are based on one of them. Terminology in this area is very confusing. The same words are used differently by different authors and managers.

Payback and Return on Investment

One of the most widely used techniques of making investment decisions is the "payback" method. The length of time required to recover the initial investment is computed and compared to the maximum payback period set by the firm. For example, an investment costing $1 million and recovering $250,000 per year has a payback period of four years. Well-informed managers will state that they understand the limitations of payback (not considering the time value of money and the cash flow pattern over the life of the investment) and that they use the payback measure more as an indication of the amount of the investment's risk (a payback of one year would indicate less risk than a payback of twenty years). Unfortunately, payback is not a reliable risk measure.

Gambling at Las Vegas, for example, may have a shorter payback period than the purchase of a U.S. Savings Bond, but gambling also has much more risk.

Another widely used method of measuring profitability of an undertaking or a project is return on investment. ROI is the average income divided by average investment for the life of the investment. Unfortunately, the ROI measure also fails to take into consideration the time value of money. The average ROI measure for the life of the asset is a very unreliable way of evaluating investments, yet there is an even worse way of applying the ROI technique. A common practice in industry is to compute the ROI of the first complete year of use. This ROI, as conventionally computed, tends to understate the actual return on investment, creating a bias against accepting investments that should be accepted.

Some corporations that understand the limitations of ROI continue to use it nevertheless. For example, the director of corporate economics of a major oil company stated: "ROI is preferred to the NPV method, in general, because the time and effort associated with changing over to an NPV system outweigh the relatively minor additional benefits (most of which are theoretical) of an NPV system." While this may be frustrating to an academic purist, it is the way that trade-offs between accuracy and cost of implementation occasionally are perceived.

The two most commonly used discounted cash flow (DCF) measures are more reliable measures of value than the payback and ROI measures described. The internal rate of return and the net present value methods are widely used, and they have a solid theoretical foundation. These techniques accomplish everything that alternative methods do, while avoiding errors introduced by these other measures.

Net Present Value

Surveys indicate that the net present value method of evaluating investments has been increasing in use since 1960. It is now difficult to find a large industrial firm that does not employ the net present value method somewhere in its organization (frequently using it in conjunction with other measures).

Once the investment's cash flows have been determined, the first step in the computation of the net present value of an investment is to choose a rate of discount (this may be a required return, or "hurdle rate"). The second step is to compute the present value equivalents of all cash flows associated with the investment (on an after-tax basis) and sum these present value equivalents to obtain the net present value of the investment. The net present value of an investment is the amount the firm could afford to pay in excess of the cost of the investment and still break even on the investment. It is also the present value of all future profits, where the profits are computed after the recovery of the capital costs of the investment.

Consider an investment costing $250,000 that promises cash flows of $130,000 one period from now and $253,500 two periods from now. Using the present value factors for $r = 0.10$, where r is the appropriate time value factor, we have the net present value shown in Table 1–2.

Table 1–2. Computing Net Present Value ($)[a]

Time Period	Cash Flows	Present Value Factors (0.10)	Present Value Equivalents
0	– 250,000	1.0000	–$250,000
1	130,000	0.9091	118,200
2	253,500	0.8264	209,500
		Net present value	$ 77,700

a. The present value factors are obtained using the formula $(1 + r)^{-n}$ where r is the discount rate and n is the number of periods until the cash is received.

The firm could pay $77,700 more than the $250,000 cost and break even (that is, it would just earn the 10 percent capital cost). Thus the $77,700 is in a sense the "excess" incentive to invest and is a measure of the safety margin that exists with this investment. The $77,700 is the increase to the shareholder's wealth as a result of accepting the project.

In the example we use the cash flows to evaluate the investment. With any required return less than 30 percent, the investment should be accepted. With a discount rate of 30 percent the NPV is equal to zero. We can evaluate the investment without reference to the accounting incomes of periods one and two. However, if incomes are computed for these periods, the present value of these incomes will be at least as large as the net present value of the cash flows (the present value of the incomes will be equal to the net present value of the cash flows if imputed interest on all capital used is deducted in computing the incomes). This conclusion is not dependent on the choice of depreciation method.

The argument is sometimes offered that the net present value method of evaluating investments is difficult to understand and to use. Actually NPV is the simplest of the procedures to use. If the net present value is positive, the investment is acceptable. Also, the interpretation of the measure is easy and useful. The net present value is the amount the firm could pay in excess of the cost and still break even, and it is the present value of the incomes *after capital costs*.

Internal Rate of Return

The net present value method yields a dollar measure. Some managers prefer a percentage measure that is most frequently called an investment's internal rate of return. Other terms applied to the same measure are yield, discounted cash flow, return on investment, time-adjusted rate of return, profitability index, and to complete the circle, present value.

We can define the internal rate of return to be that discount rate that causes the sum of the present values of the cash flows to be equal to zero. This definition then can be used to compute an investment's internal rate of return. The internal rate of return is found by a trial and error procedure (when the net present value is equal to zero, the rate of discount being used is the internal rate of return). Continuing the previous example, we find in Table 1–3 that the net present value is equal to zero using a 30 percent rate of discount. At discount rates larger than 30 percent, the net present value would be negative.

Table 1–3. Present Values with different Discount Rates

Time	r = 0 PV Factors	PV: 0.00	r = 0.40 PV Factors	PV: 0.40	r = 0.30 PV Factors	PV: 0.30
0	1.0000	−$250,000	1.0000	−$250,000	1.0000	−$250,000
1	1.0000	+130,000	0.7143	92,900	0.7692	100,000
2	1.0000	+253,500	0.5102	129,300	0.5917	150,000
NPV		+133,500		− 27,800	+	0

The internal rate of return of an investment has several interesting and relevant economic interpretations. For example, it can be described as the highest rate at which the firm can borrow, use the funds generated by the investment, and repay the loan. Assume funds are borrowed at a cost of 30 percent. The repayment schedule shown in Table 1–4 would apply.

Table 1–4. Repayment Schedule at a Cost of 30 Percent

Initial amount owed	$250,000
Year 1 interest (0.30)	+75,000
	325,000
Repayment using cash flows	130,000
	195,000
Year 2 interest (0.30)	+58,500
	253,500
Repayment using cash flows	253,500
Amount owed	0

The cash flows generated by the investment are sufficient to pay off a loan at 30 percent. If incomes and investments are measured taking time value into consideration using present value depreciation,[27] then the ROI (that is, income divided by investment) of each year will be equal to the internal rate of return of the investment. This result will not occur using conventional accounting.

The decision rule to be used with the internal rate of return method is to accept all investments with an internal rate of return greater than the required return (assuming the cash flows are those of a conventional investment; that is, one or more periods of cash outlays followed by cash inflows).

Net Present Value Profile

For any investment we can compute a net present value profile, Figure 1-1 shows the net present value profile for the previous example. Different discount rates are shown on the horizontal axis. The net present value that results from the use of the different rates of discount is shown on the vertical axis. The intersection of the net present value profile and the horizontal axis defines the internal rate of return of the investment (where the net present value is equal to zero).

Figure 1-1. Profile of Net Present Value for an Investment

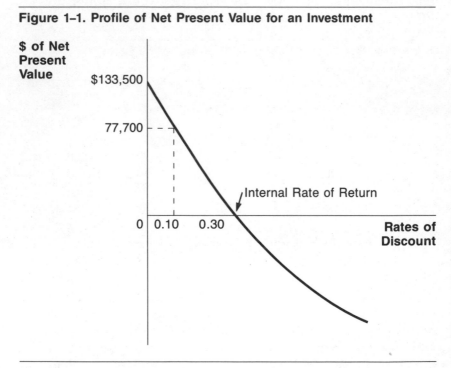

For a conventional investment (negative cash flows followed by positive), the net present value profile slopes downward to the right. For an investment with an internal rate of return greater than the required return, the net present value also will be positive. Thus with normal independent investments the net present value method (a dollar measure) and the internal rate of return method (a percentage) will give identical accept and reject decisions.

Comparing Net Present Value and Internal Rate of Return

Figure 1–2 shows why the internal rate of return and net present value methods may seem to recommend different alternatives. Assume two mutually exclusive investments A and B; the firm can accept only one of the investments.

Figure 1–2. Two Mutually Exclusive Investments

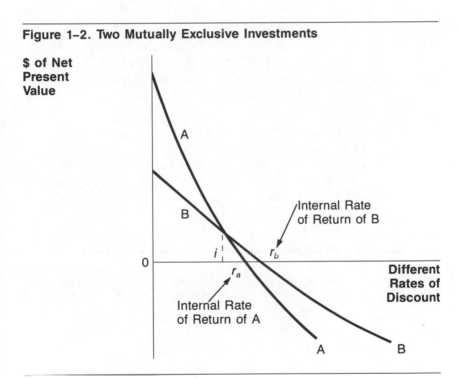

The curve AA represents the net present value profile of investment A with an internal rate of return of r_a. The intersection of the present value profile with the horizontal axis is defined to be the internal rate of return. Investment B has an internal rate of return of r_b. The net present values of the investments are measured on the vertical axis for a given rate of discount. It can be seen that B has a higher internal rate of return than A. However, for all rates of discount less than *i*, investment A has a larger net present value than investment B. Thus, if A and B are two mutually exclusive investments (only one can be undertaken), the internal rate of return criterion indicates B is preferred. The net present value method correctly indicates that A is preferred if the appropriate rate of discount is less than *i*.

If the investments are independent, and if the required return is less than r_a, then both investments are acceptable. With independent investments that have conventional cash flows (outlays followed by benefits), the internal rate of return and the net present value procedures both give consistent results. If the internal rate of return is greater than the required return, then the net present value also will be positive. If the required return is greater than the internal rate of return, the net present value is negative, and the investment is not acceptable.

Mutually Exclusive Investments

Let us assume that the firm has two mutually exclusive alternatives. The firm can modify its production process at a cost of $100,000 or replace it at a cost of $250,000. The two sets of cash flows are shown in Table 1–5.

Table 1–5. NPV for Modification versus Replacement

Time Period	Cash Flow of Modification	Cash Flow of Replacement	Incremental Flow of Replacement Minus Modification
0	−$100,000	−$250,000	−$150,000
1	+105,000	+130,000	25,000
2	+ 49,000	+253,500	204,500
IRR	0.40	0.30	0.25
NPV (0.10)	$36,000	$77,700	$41,700

The internal rate of return of modification is higher than the internal rate of return of replacement, but its net present value is less ($36,000 compared to $77,700). Figure 1–3 shows that if the appropriate time value factor is less than 25 percent (the intersection of the two curves), replacement is better than modification.

Figure 1–3. Two Mutually Exclusive Investments

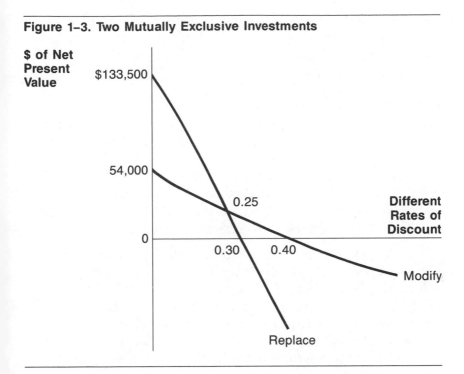

With mutually exclusive investments, the net present value method leads to reliable decisions. The internal rate of return approach is not reliable unless the incremental cash flows are computed and the internal rate of return of these flows is computed (this is the 0.25 marked on Figure 1–3).

The Assumptions

The analysis using either the net present value or the internal rate of return method gives exact answers if assumptions implicit in the calculations are valid. The first necessary assumption is that the cash flows are known with certainty. There is no need to adjust for risk. The second assumption is that we can lend and borrow at one given rate of interest. This implies that all the capital needed to undertake the desirable investments can be obtained at the same borrowing rate. The third assumption is that investments can be accepted or rejected based on their overall economic worth (it is not necessary to consider short-run consequences). A fourth assumption is trivial, but should be noted. It is assumed that the cash flows are received at the end of each period and a discrete discount for time formulation (the formula $(1 + r)^{-n}$) can be used. This assumption can be dropped without harming the basic analysis and conclusions.

Relaxing the Assumptions

The four assumptions above enable us to evaluate investment alternatives using the relatively straightforward discounted cash flow methods. But even if the assumptions are dropped, the basic preferred method of calculation will still be a DCF method. For example, one of the more widely used methods of coping with uncertain cash flows is to increase the required return (the hurdle rate). This adjustment is certainly in the right direction.

If the borrowing rate is higher than the lending rate, and if the firm is borrowing, a common practice is to assume the firm will be in a borrowing position throughout the life of the asset. While this is not exactly accurate if there will be periods in which the firm will be in a lending status, it is a sensible pragmatic approach to what otherwise would be a difficult conceptual problem (an even worse problem would be getting the necessary information for more exact solutions).

Strategy Considerations

What is the relationship of the capital budgeting techniques described in this chapter and the issue of overall business strategy? If there were no uncertainty, all investment decisions could be made reliably using one of the discounted cash flow methods. With uncertainty of cash flows and of interactions between projects, there are strategy considerations affecting the choice of projects for many firms. We need to consider how, if at all, strategy factors should affect the choice of investments.

A Problem of Implementation

Once a company has decided on a DCF method, there still remains the problem of installing the system. Too often the educational program starts at the bottom, with top management expected to learn the system by a magical osmosis. The difficulties in installing a system were noted by one executive as follows: "Initially, the principal impediment is overcoming resistance to change and galvanizing organization-wide understanding and commitment. Firm support from one's CEO, coupled with educating non-financial managers about present value, cost of capital, capital rationing, etc., are vital at this juncture."

Conclusions

It should be emphasized that the net present value and internal rate of return methods are theoretically correct methods that—used correctly—can assist managers in their attempts to make better capital budgeting decisions. These methods do not replace a manager's judgment, but rather are an effective way of implementing judgment.

As we relax the certainty assumption, we will find that the absolutely correct and definite decision rules for accepting or rejecting investments will become less definite and that management's judgment calls are required. In later chapters we will relax the assumption that the cash flows are known with certainty and will investigate the situation called "capital rationing" (the firm has more projects than capital available for investment). One survey respondent commented, "Our greatest difficulty is in controlling the assumptions used initially to justify capital projects. We find that if we make poor decisions, it is because the assumptions were wrong, not because our budgeting techniques were improperly designed or poorly implemented."

Note 28 lists relevant journals and notes 29–45 list additional journal articles for readers who would like to enlarge their understanding of the issues discussed in this chapter. Notes 46–58 list additional books dealing with capital budgeting issues.

2

Capital Budgeting and Risk

The Discount Rate

> *Implementing capital budgeting techniques depends on judgment and foresight of those looking into the future. Sophisticated analysis seldom compensates for bad judgment.*
> *A Vice President, Finance*

The remark of the finance officer quoted above describes a common viewpoint that has persisted among managers since discounted cash flow methods were first introduced in the business literature in the 1950s. No one would argue in favor of "bad judgment," and everyone would agree that good judgment is essential for good investment decisions. But once judgment has been used to define the cash flows, good sophisticated analysis will increase the likelihood of making desirable decisions. The existence of uncertainty is not a valid justification for using techniques that are known to be deficient.

There are two basic problems we need to solve when uncertainty is introduced into the investment analysis. The first is to estimate the cash flows of each period and their probability distributions. The second problem is to compute or estimate a risk-adjusted net present value of these flows. To solve this second problem we have to take into consideration both the time value of money and risk. In this chapter we will consider the basic issue of how uncertainty should be incorporated in decisionmaking.

Gitman and Forrester found that 64.3 percent of the firms responding to their survey identified "project definition and cash flow estimation" to be the most difficult and most important stage of capital budgeting.[1] When there is uncertainty as to cash flows, one common solution is to adjust the discount rate upward.

The results of the survey conducted for this book are consistent with the findings of Gitman and Forrester. A large percentage of the responses referred to the problems of determining cash flows and choosing the discount rate. Typical statements were the following, the first by an assistant treasurer of a corporation and the second by a corporate director of business development.

Any capital project has an element of risk that should be considered as part of the evaluation. The assessment of risk becomes difficult when the diverse businesses of an integrated oil company are considered.

The economic value of capital projects that involve lead times of three to five years varies substantially with different price scenarios. Our capital budgeting forecasts frequently are based on data that are subject to great volatility. We try to anticipate events but are not always successful.

Uncertain Cash Flows

The two easiest solutions to the problem of uncertain cash flows are to use the most likely cash flow for a period or to use the expected value of the period's cash flow. In computing the present value or the yield of a bond, the conventional practice is to use the contractual cash flows. Contractual cash flows are also the most likely cash flows. The use of most likely cash flows does not have a great deal of theoretical justification, but the method is a convenient calculation, and it is widely used.

The second method is to use the expected value of the cash flows for each period. This procedure has the virtue of taking into consideration all possible values and their probabilities, not just the most likely value.

Assume the following possible outcomes are projected for period one cash flows:

Event	Probability	Outcome	Expectation
e_1	0.1	$-\$4,000$	$-\$ 400$
e_2	0.4	$+ 1,000$	400
e_3	0.3	$+ 6,000$	1,800
e_4	0.2	$+11,000$	2,200
		Expected value	$\$ 4,000$

The most likely outcome (40 percent chance) is $1,000. The expected value is $4,000. The difficulty of using the most likely outcome is highlighted by the fact that we could change any outcome except event e_2 (plus $1,000) without changing the value of the most likely event unless the probability of the outcome changed was greater than 40 percent. One might not want to make a decision based solely on the use of expected monetary value, but equally important is the fact that we would not want to make a decision without knowing the expected monetary value of the investment.

The decisionmaker should want to know the spread of outcomes. For example, it is useful to know that the least desirable event that can occur at the end of the period is a loss of $4,000.

A commonly used measure to summarize the spread of outcomes is the variance of the distribution. To compute the variance of the period one cash flows, we subtract the expected value from each possible outcome, square the difference, and compute the expected value of the squared differences. With the above set of outcomes, the variance is $21,000,000. The variance is zero if one outcome has a probability of one.

Event	Outcome	(Outcome −$4,000)	(Outcome −$4,000)²	Probability	Probability Times (Outcome −$4,000)²
e_1	−$4,000	−$8,000	64×10^6	0.1	6.4×10^6
e_2	+ 1,000	− 3,000	9×10^6	0.4	3.6×10^6
e_3	+ 6,000	+ 2,000	4×10^6	0.3	1.2×10^6
e_4	+11,000	+ 7,000	49×10^6	0.2	9.8×10^6
					21×10^6

Simulation

In some situations a mathematical solution would be too complex, and the decisionmaker finds it convenient to use a simulation technique to arrive at a solution. A form of simulation is to use a Monte Carlo approach. Probability distributions are estimated for the uncertain outcomes. One outcome is drawn for each uncertain event. Putting all the outcomes together we have one trial. For example, assume the possible outcomes for the outlay at time zero associated with the time one cash flows described above are

Event	Probability	Outcome	Expectation
s_1	0.2	−$5,000	−$1,000
s_2	0.5	− 3,000	− 1,500
s_3	0.3	− 1,000	− 300
		Expected value	−$2,800

To simulate the initial outlay we can draw a number from one to ten where

s_1 occurs if either 1 or 2 is drawn   (probability = 0.2)
s_2 occurs if either 3, 4, 5, 6, or 7 is drawn (probability = 0.5)
s_3 occurs if either 8, 9, or 10 is drawn (probability = 0.3)

The process is repeated for period one's cash flows, but now we have

e_1 occurs if 1 is drawn on the second (probability = 0.1)
    lottery
e_2 occurs if 2, 3, 4, or 5 is drawn (probability = 0.4)
e_3 occurs if 6, 7, or 8 is drawn (probability = 0.3)
e_4 occurs if 9 or 10 is drawn (probability = 0.2)

For example, if number 2 is drawn first and then 8 we would have

Time	Event	Cash Flows
0	s_1	− $5,000
1	e_3	+ 6,000

This is one trial. The process would be repeated many times to derive a probabiltiy distribution of outcomes. The manager makes the decision using this distribution. Hertz describes this type of analysis in detail in his 1964 *Harvard Business Review* article.[2] But Brigham warned in 1975 that "data problems may, however, keep Hertz-type simulation from ever being widely used in industry."[3] Estimation of the future cash flows and their probability distributions remains a major problem. Simulation is helpful, but it does not offer the perfect solution to the uncertainty problem. Judgment is still a necessary ingredient.

Sensitivity Analysis

With sensitivity analysis the values of parameters are changed to test the effect of the changes on the final result. For example, what effect is there if unit sales are reduced 10 percent? What happens if labor costs are increased by 15 percent?

Sensitivity analysis is a very useful way of estimating the amount of risk. For example, assume it is thought that the maximum possible shrinkage in sales is 20 percent. If there is still a positive net present value if sales shrink to this level, then we have determined that a 20 percent shrinkage of sales is not the primary concern.

To use sensitivity analysis, generally one changes the value of one variable and holds all else constant. If this does not seem to be an appropriate approach, it is possible to use a simulation technique, which is more powerful. With either approach, the output is a large number of possible outcomes that then must be evaluated.

Survey Results

Petty and Bowlin reported in 1976 that 33.6 percent of the firms they surveyed used simulation.[4] Gitman and Mercurio found in 1982 that 37.9 percent of the firms responding used sensitivity analysis and 20.9 percent used simulation.[5] Thus a significant percentage of the firms surveyed use some type of modeling technique.

Many managers say that they use these techniques and generate a large amount of data, but that they do not know how to use the information once they get it. There are two analytical problems in looking at such information. One involves the choice of the rate of discount to evaluate each trial, and the second is, if one obtains a distribution of net present values (or of internal rates of return), what does one do to turn the probability distribution into a decision? We do not have exactly correct solutions for either of these two problems, but we do know that there are calculations for time value and risk that give useful insights.

Coping with Risk

The Discount Rate

The discount rate used by corporations can vary over a wide range of choices. Among them are

- Default-free rate that can be earned on invested funds (after tax)
- Debt borrowing rate (after tax) either of issuing new debt or retiring old debt
- Weighted average cost of capital (with the cost of new equity capital possibly being different from the cost of retained earnings)
- Risk-adjusted discount rates for each project
- Risk-adjusted discount rates for each division

All these techniques are used in industry. Table 2–1 reproduces a table that Gitman and Forrester present. The fact that approximately one-half of the firms responding adjust the rate of discount for risk is important. An adjustment is desirable, but understanding that the amount of adjustment must be of reasonable magnitude is equally important.

The table lumps together expected values of cash flows and certainty equivalents. Following the logic of this chapter, we would distinguish between the two.

Table 2–1. Methods Used to Adjust for Risk and Uncertainty

Method	Number of Responses	Percent of Responses
Increase the minimum rate of return or cost of capital	44	42.7
Use expected values of cash flows (certainty-equivalents)	27	26.2
Subjective adjustment of cash flows	19	18.5
Decrease minimum payback period	13	12.6
Total responses	103	100.0

Source: L.J. Gitman and J.R. Forrester, Jr., "A Survey of Capital Budgeting Techniques Used by Major U.S. Firms," *Financial Management* (Fall 1977): 66–71.

The Basic Problem

The basic problem is that both risk and timing must be considered. It is not likely that risk and timing will combine nicely into an easy mathematical relationship (such as the present value factor $(1 + r)^{-n}$) to translate a risky future cash flow into a present value equivalent. Let us assume a $1 million investment that leads to the following two outcomes being possible at time one:

Outcome	Dollars	Probability	Expected Value
e_1	$2,500,000	0.5	$1,250,000
e_2	0	0.5	0
		Expected value	$1,250,000

Using the expected value of the cash flows, we obtain an internal rate of return of 25 percent. Assume that as the investor we find this investment has a risk-adjusted net present value of zero and is only marginally desirable, even though the best we can earn on government securities is 10 percent and it only costs us 10 percent to borrow. With the proposed investment there is a 50 percent probability of losing $1 million, and risk aversion reduces the present value of the benefits to $1 million.

The present value of expected positive cash flows using 10 percent as the discount rate is

$$\frac{\$1,250,000}{1.10} = \$1,136,364.$$

As the risk-adjusted present value (and the most we will pay) is $1 million, there is a $136,364 adjustment for risk. The risk-adjusted net present value is equal to zero.

An alternative solution is to say that while 10 percent represents the discount rate for a project without significant risk, we would use 25 percent to evaluate this investment given the amount of risk. The use of 25 percent as the discount rate leads to a risk-adjusted present value of $1 million—that is

$$\frac{\$1,250,000}{1.25} = \$1,000,000$$

and a zero net present value.

So far we can use either of two solutions:

1. Adjust the discount rate from 10 to 25 percent. The investment is marginally desirable. The investor is indifferent between undertaking and not undertaking the investment.
2. Subtract a $136,364 adjustment for risk from the net present value computed using the default-free rate of 10 percent. Again, the investment is marginally desirable. The $136,364 is equal to $150,000 $(1.10)^{-1}$.

Now assume we have the same investment outcomes, but assume they take place at time ten rather than at time one. Using the risk-adjusted rate of 25 percent applied to the expected value of the cash flows, we obtain

$$\$1,250,000 \ (1.25)^{-10} = \$134,218.$$

If we discount the cash flows for time using 10 percent discount rate, we obtain

$$\$1,250,000\ (1.10)^{-10} = \$481,929.$$

But if we use 10 percent as the discount rate, it is necessary to subtract an adjustment for risk from the $481,929 present value. How much should be subtracted? To better understand the issue requires another concept, the certainty equivalent.

The Certainty Equivalent

Consistent with the preceding example, let us now assume that if the investment paid off immediately (rather than at the end of one year or at the end of ten years), it would have a value of $1,100,000. That is, investors would be indifferent between accepting $1,100,000 and a chance to win $2,500,000 or obtain $0 (each with a 50 percent probability). A risk adjustment of $150,000 is subtracted from the $1,250,000 expected monetary value.

If the payoff takes place at time one rather than at time zero, the present value of the $1,100,000 of certainty equivalent would be

$$\frac{\$1,100,000}{1.10} = \$1,000,000.$$

and the investment again is marginally acceptable.

Now assume the payoff is at time ten. Immediately before the value of the uncertain payoff is revealed, its certainty equivalent value is $1,100,000. The present value of this certainty equivalent using the default-free rate is $1,100,000 $(1.10)^{-10} = \$424,098$.

An equivalent calculation is to discount $1,250,000 at 10 percent and then subtract the present value of the $150,000 risk adjustment.

$$\$1,250,000\ (1.10)^{-10} = \$481,929 \quad \text{present value without any risk adjustment}$$
$$150,000\ (1.10)^{-10} = \underline{\quad 57,831} \quad \text{present value of risk adjustment}$$
$$\$424,098 \quad \text{present value of payoffs (risk-adjusted)}$$

Now we have two different risk-adjusted present values. Using the risk-adjusted discount rate method and a discount rate of 25 percent, we obtain $134,218. Computing the present value without risk and then subtracting a dollar risk adjustment, we obtain $424,098. Which is the better estimate of value to use?

To emphasize the deficiency of the risk-adjusted discount rate as a general tool, let us assume that immediately before time ten the payoff can be bought or sold for its certainty equivalent of $1,100,000. Thus the value will be $1,100,000 at time ten immediately before the outcome is determined. We have stated that the firm can borrow at 10 percent. If at time zero it borrows $424,098 at 10 percent, at time ten the investor will owe

$$\$424,098 \ (1.10)^{10} \ = \ \$1,100,000.$$

Paying $424,098 for the investment the investor breaks even. But using the risk-adjusted discount rate, we obtained a value of only $134,218. Thus if the investment could be purchased for $200,000, the alternative would be rejected incorrectly, based on the $134,218 of benefits. If the $200,000 is borrowed, at time ten the firm will owe

$$\$200,000 \ (1.10)^{10} \ = \ \$518,748.$$

Financed with borrowed funds, the $200,000 investment would lead to a debt obligation of $518,748 at time ten, but the value of the investment at that time is the certainty equivalent of $1,100,000. A firm should be willing to pay as much as $424,098 for the investment, although obviously it would prefer to pay less.

The certainty equivalent approach clearly dominates the risk-adjusted discount rate approach in this example. However, two very important observations should be made. First, while the 25 percent risk-adjusted discount rate is correct when the payoff is at time one, it is not correct when the cash flows (with the identical risk) occur at any other time. To use the risk-adjusted discount rate method correctly would require reducing the discount rate from 25 percent to a lower value. With the same risk, cash flows occurring at different periods should be adjusted at different discount rates.

Second, while we consistently used a certainty equivalent of $1,100,000 in the example, in the real world the systematic reliable determination of certainty equivalents is not feasible. While in concept a highly desirable approach, in practice the certainty equivalent method falls short, because we do not know how to determine systematically and reliably certainty equivalents of cash flows occurring through time.

It is not always wrong to use the same rate for different time periods, because it is possible that risk will increase through time. Assume that at time ten the expected value is again $1,250,000, but the certainty equivalent is now only $348,126 (risk increasing through time). Discounting the expected value by 25 percent, we obtain

$$\$1,250,000 \ (1.25)^{-10} \ = \ \$134,218.$$

Discounting the $348,126 certainty equivalent at 10 percent, we obtain

$$\$348,126 \ (1.10)^{-10} \ = \ \$134,218.$$

Now the use of the 25 percent discount rate for both the time one lottery and the time ten lottery is reasonable. If the risk increases through time, there is some possibility that the use of a risk-adjusted discount rate will give reasonable results.

In practice, firms tend to use relatively uncomplicated discount rate measures. Thus, Schall, Sundem, and Geijsbeek found that 17 percent of the firms reporting use the cost of debt, 46 percent use the weighted average cost of capital, and 9 percent use the cost of equity capital.[6] Brigham concluded after a survey of thirty-three large corporations that "although 94 percent of the sample firms use DCF methodology, only 62 percent use a hurdle rate based on the cost of capital, only 53 percent use more than one hurdle rate (in spite of admitted risk differentials among projects), and less than half change their hurdle rates even once a year."[7]

Bower and Jenks introduce the important fact that an asset's risk characteristics affect the asset's contribution to the firm's debt capacity and this factor should affect its risk-adjusted discount rate.[8] Taggart,[9] Myers,[10] and Hong and Rappaport[11] also bring together the financing decision and the cost of capital for the capital budgeting decision being made.

We have not considered whether or not it makes a difference if we know the outcome of the investment at time zero or time ten if the investment's payoff is at time ten. Epstein and Turnbull study this question, but their conclusions are too complex to be applied easily in industry.[12]

The Capital Asset Pricing Model (CAPM)

The CAPM uses the risk-return opportunities of the capital market to determine the required return for any investment. One of the assumptions of the CAPM is that all the securities in the market are fairly priced, with the result that the market is in equilibrium. By investing in all securities (there are no transaction costs) the investor succeeds in eliminating all non–market-related risk. The non–market-related risk (also called residual or nonsystematic risk) for each firm is assumed to be independent. As only a very small amount is invested in each security (the investor is perfectly diversified), this residual risk goes to zero for the investor.

Consider a gamble where there are two possible outcomes:

Event	Probability	Outcome
e_1	0.5	100
e_2	0.5	-80

The expected value is $10 but there is a 50 percent probability of losing $80. Now assume that we split the investment between two independent gambles and the outcomes are as shown in Figure 2–1.

The equally likely outcomes of the second gamble are independent of whether e_1 or e_2 occurs. The probability of the $80 loss has been reduced from 50 to 25 percent. Further splitting of the investment among other identical independent investments would drive the probability of the loss lower. With a very large number of splits, the probability of the loss would approach zero. With the CAPM this type of risk is called residual or unsystematic risk and is assumed to be zero because the investor is well diversified.

Figure 2-1. Outcomes for Two Independent Gambles

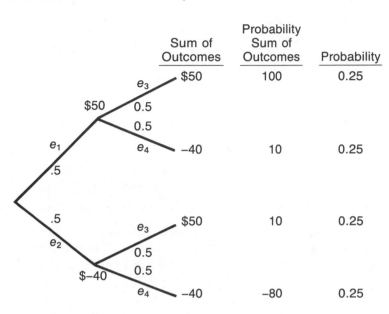

	Sum of Outcomes	Probability Sum of Outcomes	Probability
e_3	$50	100	0.25
e_4	−40	10	0.25
e_3	$50	10	0.25
e_4	−40	−80	0.25

There are some authors who are willing to bet that the CAPM offers a workable solution to the problem of coping with uncertainty. Mullins[13] and Weston[14] offer excellent summaries and evaluations of the CAPM, concluding that it is useful. Weston states, "the Capital Asset Pricing Model permits the criteria for asset expansion decisions to be set out unambiguously and compactly."[15] However, the conventional CAPM model has the following limitations:

♦ The basic assumptions of the model (including the assumption that only the mean and variance of an investment portfolio are relevant; this assumption is reasonable if the probability distribution of outcomes is normal or if a special assumption is made concerning risk preferences).
♦ Estimating the premium of the expected market return over the default-free rate is difficult.
♦ The estimation of the default-free rate does not lead to one exact value because the value will depend on the time until maturity.

◆ The measure of the systematic risk is not stable through time.

But the most important limitation is that the CAPM considers only systematic risk and leaves out unsystematic (project, division, or firm-specific) risk. Managers and undiversified investors want unsystematic risk to be considered. There are very few managers who want to use a discount rate that adjusts for systematic risk but leaves out the unique risks of the asset. While academics can state that well-diversified investors need only adjust for systematic risk, the fact is that unsystematic risk is a relevant factor for managers. Managers are likely to act in a manner that considers unsystematic risk. They are typically not perfectly diversified—given that one of their major assets is their career.

Petty and Bowlin found that only 2.2 percent of the firms surveyed indicated they used the CAPM.[16] (To place this percentage in perspective, 76.5 percent of the firms indicated that they used discounted cash flows.) However, Gitman and Mercurio found 21.5 percent used the CAPM (35 percent used some form of risk-adjusted discount rate method).[17] Myers and Turnbull,[18] Fama,[19] and Rendleman[20] have all offered insightful explanations of the limitations of the CAPM as a means of making capital budgeting decisions.

Risk-Adjusted Rates
One can accept a hypothesis that operating units with more risk should be expected to earn a larger return. This leads many firms to the logical conclusion that each division should have a required return (or hurdle rate) that reflects the risk of the division. Thus we have a manager of financial planning stating: "We basically employ a Capital Asset Pricing Model approach to estimating cost of equity by risk category of business (risk-free rate plus market equity risk premium adjusted by the appropriate Beta)."

The omission of unsystematic risk seems to be accepted by this firm. We do not know if operating managers of the firm accept the fact that it is omitted. A second firm adjusts the amount of debt leverage for each of its "risk categories":

Our Treasury Department determines hurdle rates for the seven major categories" of business in which the company participates. The company's overall cost of debt is imputed to each business with the amount of leverage varied according to risk among the seven categories. A cost of equity is determine individually for each category (like leverage) generally consistent with independent A-rated competitors.

Correctly adjusting the discount rate for the risk of an operating unit is more an art than a science.

Frequency of Revision

How frequently should a firm adjust its discount rate? The manager of financial planning of one firm argues for one year but is not at ease with the choice.

As we are continually making investment decisions, practicality dictates that the hurdle rates possess stability, and we try to revise them no more than once each year. Although the cost of debt assumption used in the hurdle rates is our best judgment of the long-term rate expected over the two to three-year financing period for most of our projects, the volatility of the capital markets in recent years has resulted in frequent concern as to the efficacy of our hurdle rates at any given time.

Theoretically the hurdle rate should reflect the current costs of raising capital. Practical problems are likely to limit the number of times a year the hurdle rate can be revised, but management should work toward the goal that the discount rate being used reflects the current costs of using capital.

The Discount Rate and Taxes

We know that if debt costs 14 percent per year and if the marginal corporate tax rate is 34 percent, the after-tax cost of debt is

$$(1 - 0.34)0.14 = 0.0924.$$

But what if the firm is not paying taxes now and does not expect to pay taxes in the future? An extreme example of this situation is described by a corporate controller:

We are in an interesting situation for capital budgeting, and it represents something of a quandary. Past losses will prevent us from paying any appreciable income tax for many years to come. Normally, this would mean that our pretax discount rate would be relaxed by one-half, since it becomes equivalent to our after-tax rate. But it seems inconsistent for a company in financial trouble to accept propositions now which would have been unacceptable when times are better.

What does financial theory say about hurdle rates for companies in tax loss carryforward positions?

If the corporation were not to pay taxes for the entire planning horizon, then the debt rate would be equal to the before-tax borrowing rate (0.14 in the example above). This higher rate makes it more difficult to accept projects. However, the cash flows should reflect the tax loss carryforwards. These make it easier to accept an investment. For the problem cited by the controller above, there could be an easy answer. Assume that a firm borrows at k; so its after-tax cost is $(1 - t)k$, where t is its tax rate. Also, if it earns X before tax, then it will earn $(1 - t)X$ after tax. With a constant cash flow (a perpetuity) we have

$$PV = \frac{(1 - t)X}{(1 - t)k} = \frac{X}{k}.$$

The before- and after-tax measures of PV are equal. With finite-lived assets the results are not so neat. But we do have both the cash flows and the discount rate affected. Given that a firm that is not taxed keeps the $1 that is earned (there is no tax), it is not unreasonable that such a firm might accept investments that another firm being taxed would reject. The before-tax cost of equity capital is less for a firm not being taxed than for a firm that is taxed.

We can conclude that the tax rate for a specific firm affects both the discount rate and the cash flow calculation. A change in a firm's status will affect the discount rate. One fact remains constant, however. It is the marginal tax rate that is relevant for a firm, not the average rate. (This recommendation may be easier to state than it is to follow in practice.)

But Decisions Must Be Made

Assume a situation where cash flows and their timing and probability distributions are fed into a computer, a button is pushed, and the optimum decision is revealed. No judgment would be required. This is not the case in the present real world. All we can do is make a series of reasonable calculations for each investment and evaluate the entire set of information. Among the things that should be calculated are

- ◆ The net present value profile (rather than relying on one net present value measure)
- ◆ The internal rate of return (while part of the net present value profile, this measure is important in its own right)
- ◆ The net present value profile for different assumptions (sensitivity analysis)

Many firms cope with uncertainty by computing several different measures. For example, the assistant treasurer of one firm explained: "We use several different financial measures in evaluating investment proposals including internal rate of return (IRR), discounted payback, profitability index, and "proof year" operating return on investment. The greatest weight is accorded to IRR in most cases."

The most important step to avoid is the making of investment decisions using a single measure, such as a very large risk-adjusted discount rate, for a wide range of types of investment. We do not know how to choose one correct risk adjusted rate for many different multiperiod assets.

Conclusions

It is important that managers realize that the academic community does not have easy exact ways of making "accept" or "reject" decisions for large independent investments with large amounts of risk. Judgment must be used to complement the objective quantitative measures of invesment worth. We can conclude that if we hold all things equal except for risk, the higher the risk, the higher the required return. But this is not a very useful conclusion except in the case of specialized investments such as bonds, since all other things are rarely equal.

The spirit of this chapter and its recommendation was captured by an assistant treasurer who states "in the end, however, there is no way to achieve a situation in which project returns, individually or on average, can be compared with assurance to the cost-of-capital benchmark. Capital budgeting is, and will remain, an art as opposed to a science."

Acceptance of the premise that capital budgeting is an art does not change the conclusion that the tools that are known today, properly applied, can improve investment decisionmaking.

The most dramatic of the statements concerning uncertainty was made by an executive making investments for productive capacity for products not yet designed:

In addition to organizational complexity, we are faced with capital budgeting lead times for new technology capacity that often exceed the horizon of our strategic planning process for individual products. Occasionally, we are investing in capacity to house machinery and equipment that has not been invented that will produce products not yet on the drawing boards of the product development divisions. Clearly, the uncertainties and risks of this environment make analytical analysis of capital budgeting an art at best.

Further references on capital budgeting and risk are listed in notes 21–39.

3

Estimating Cash Flows for Investment Analysis

Another problem, not only of implementation but one which requires ongoing vigilance, is the need to develop the best possible estimate of incremental cash flows which would result from undertaking an investment.

A Chief Financial Officer

Many firms consider the estimation of cash flows to be the major problem in implementing capital investment decisions. For example, a treasurer states: "Academics spend a lot of time developing analyses to determine the correct rate at which to discount cash flows for making investment decisions. In implementing capital investment techniques here, this was not an important issue. It is the determination of the relevant cash flows that is most important to implementing these techniques."

The determination of cash flows is a primary problem in successful implementation of capital budgeting techniques. While we can do a very good job of defining the cash flows to be included and excluded, the analyst still faces the problem of inserting specific numbers to reflect benefits and costs of a project. Consider two investment alternatives, one by an oil company to make an investment to increase the yield from an oil field, and the second by a public utility to build a nuclear electric generating plant.

To evaluate the oil field investment, the firm needs to know

◆ Future oil prices and consumption
◆ Future costs of recovery
◆ Future transportation costs for oil
◆ Future tax rates
◆ Future interest rates
◆ The rate at which the oil can be recovered (pumped)
◆ The total amount of oil to be recovered
◆ Future government regulation and controls

This is an impressive list in itself, but consider what is needed in the case of the nuclear generating plant. In addition to several of the items above, some of the factors to be considered are

◆ Oil and coal prices and availability (competitive energy sources)
◆ The ten-year lead time that it takes to get a plant built
◆ Changing construction and safety requirements imposed by the various governments
◆ Waste disposal costs and costs of closing the plant at the end of life
◆ Demand for electricity for ten to forty years
◆ The return allowed by the regulatory commissions
◆ Consequences of an accident or shutdown of operations
◆ Availability of capital to complete the plant (including regulatory treatment of construction work in progress)
◆ The reaction of the stock market to the capital expenditure and the quality of earnings (complicated by the presence of an allowance for funds used during construction)
◆ Possible future changes in the way the industry is organized (such as cogeneration of electricity)

The list of factors to be considered for any investment is long. The primary fact to be recognized is the presence and importance of uncertainty. Cash flows for any investment project are going to be estimates. They may be based on expert judgment, but they are estimates nevertheless.

Cash Flow Estimation

Optimism

Managers in many firms face the problem of excessively optimistic cash flow estimates. Need for project approval is one factor that causes optimistic forecasts. An assistant treasurer stated:

If project analysts typically view future uncertainties in an optimistic light, however, which can happen when a company has limited funds to invest and proposed investments are being considered on a competitive basis, then projects which do better than forecast may be less common than short-fall projects. Overly optimistic forecasting has been a continuing challenge in capital budgeting.

One common solution to balance optimistic cash flow forecasts is to increase the hurdle rate to compensate for the biased cash flow inputs. Thus we have the following from another assistant treasurer: "Various approaches are available to offset optimistic forecasting, none a panacea. Hurdle rates in excess of the Cost of Capital can be required for projects to leave a 'margin for error', unfortunately, this practice may encourage even more optimistic forecasting."

Cash Flow Calculation and Presentation

The following are some important factors to consider in preparing cash flow projections (they are based on all the responses from the financial officers surveyed, but one corporate vice president made a significant contribution to the list):

- ◆ Clarify all assumptions so that the projections are supported by either facts or reasonable hypotheses.
- ◆ Indicate the effect of the product being considered on other products of the firm.
- ◆ Exclude sink costs, but
- ◆ Include opportunity costs for any factor of production even if there is not an explicit cash outlay.

◆ Exclude allocated overheads that will not change, but include overheads that will change.
◆ Ensure that the tax rate used reflects future marginal tax effects.
◆ Exclude all financing flows including the tax shield of interest (it will be included in the discount rate).
◆ Include the net working capital that is needed.
◆ Include the asset's entire life in the analysis.

While cash flows should be used in the evaluation of investments, one can use income measures as long as the interest on all capital used is deducted in computing the income.

Relevant Cash Flows

Only incremental cash flows are included in the cash flow stream. One particularly difficult area is in the treatment of overhead allocations. Assume a company has an overhead rate of $20 per direct labor hour. In evaluating a new project, or the abandonment of a current project, this $20 overhead rate cannot be used. A study must be made as to the amount of overhead that will be incurred as a result of the project, or saved when a current project is abandoned. The typical overhead rate is an average cost calculation that cannot be used for incremental decisions.

An analogous problem arises when currently used assets have excess capacity, and a decision has to be made whether the cost of these assets should affect a new project if the new project will make use of these assets. As the cost of these assets is a sunk cost, it is not relevant to the analysis to decide whether or not to accept a new project. On the other hand, if there are alternative uses for currently used assets, the value of these competitive uses is relevant. Opportunity costs (the values of alternative uses) are always relevant.

A third cash flow identification problem arises in a decision to abandon or sell currently used assets. The cost of these assets is not relevant to the economic analysis, except to the extent that their cost affects the firm's tax position. While the sunk cost is not relevant, any alternative use does affect the analysis, for it defines a minimum price that has to be obtained.

Calculation of Cash Flows

Several troublesome items complicate cash flow calculation. One complexity involves changes in working capital. If more net working capital is needed because of the new project, then more total capital is needed, and this is a use of cash. A decrease in net working capital needed is an inflow of cash, because capital is being released that can be used for other purposes.

A second complexity comes from treatment of financing flows associated with the investment. The easiest solution is to omit all financing flows and analyze only the investment flows. Common errors are to include interest, include the tax shield of interest, and include lease flows. These errors are likely to distort decisionmaking.

For some purposes, all debt flows and their tax effects are included. The result is a stock equity cash flow rather than the conventional investment cash flow. The problem with including all debt flows is that it is difficult to define the return that is necessary. The amount of debt that is included helps determine the return that is required, and the amount of debt is likely to vary throughout the life of the investment. Inclusion of some debt flows is an error, and inclusion of all the debt flows makes it difficult to evaluate the internal rate of return or the net present value of the investment.

While depreciation expense and other expenses not using cash do not directly affect the cash flow calculation, depreciation influences the income tax paid, so tax depreciation expense does affect the cash flow stream.

Cash Flow Analysis and Accounting

The analysis of investments should be accomplished using the cash flows of the investments. The objective of the analysis is to determine if it is worthwhile to undertake the project. The accounting process uses the rules of accrual accounting to determine how the firm performed in each time period. Conventional accounting can create a bias against a desirable investment if the analyst is concerned with the operating results of one or two years rather than with the economic impact of the project over its entire life.

Consider an investment with the following projected cash flows:

Time	Cash Flow
0	-$3,000
1	1,200
2	1,440
3	1,728

The investment's internal rate of return is 20 percent and the investment is desirable for any discount rate less than 20 percent. Now let us consider the incomes and returns on investment that result from the use of conventional accounting and straight-line depreciation.

Period	Revenue	Straight-Line Depreciation	Income	Book Investment	ROI
1	$1,200	$1,000	$200	$3,000	0.067
2	1,440	1,000	440	2,000	0.220
3	1,728	1,000	728	1,000	0.728

The ROI of year one is not adequate given the 20 percent required return. If management is concerned with short-run operating performance as measured by the accountant, the investment would be rejected. A solution is to define the depreciation expense to be the change in present value of the investment using the internal rate of return as the discount rate (this is present value or economic depreciation).

Period	Revenue	Depreciation	Income	Beginning Investment	ROI
1	$1,200	$ 600	$600	$3,000	0.20
2	1,440	960	480	2,400	0.20
3	1,728	1,440	288	1,440	0.20

Depreciation Calculation	
The value at time 0 is 3,000	3,000 − 2,400 = 600
The value at time 1 is 2,400	2,400 − 1,440 = 960
The value at time 2 is 1,440	1,440 − 0 = 1,440
The value at time 3 is 0	

With economic depreciation, each period has an ROI equal to the project's internal rate of return. There is not necessarily a conflict between the investment decisionmaking process and the accounting performance measures.

Taxes

Both the cash flows and the discount rate have to be on an after-tax basis. Revenues and out-of-pocket expenses are both multiplied by $(1 - t)$ where t is the relevant tax rate for the period. Let us assume that the current corporate tax rate is 34 percent. Then $(1 - 0.34)$ would be used for those periods where the current tax rate is expected to apply.

If the firm currently pays a tax that is only 20 percent of the accounting income, the firm has to compute the marginal tax rate. Even though the tax rate computed as an average of the accounting income is only 20 percent, the marginal tax rate can still be 34 percent.

To illustrate why the average tax rate is a bad measure to use, assume a tax law allowing a 10 percent investment tax credit that if taken reduces the asset's tax basis by 5 percent. Assume that without the investment the firm would pay $100 of taxes at time zero. (For simplicity, we will assume these facts apply even if the life of the asset is one year, and we will assume a tax credit can reduce a corporate tax to zero.)

Assume an asset costing $1,000 will lead to a $100 invest-ment tax credit now, and before-tax cash flows of $1,010.61 at time one. While the corporation will save more taxes than it will pay, it is correct to use a 34 percent tax rate in evaluating the investment. The initial investment is $900 (the $1,000 cost minus the $100 ITC). The after-tax cash flows at time one are

$$\$1,010.61 \ (1 - 0.34) + 950 \ (0.34) = 667 + 323 = \$990.$$

The $990 is a 10 percent return on the effective investment of $900. The tax (at time one) is

$$Tax = (\$1,010.61 - 950)\ 0.34 = 20.61,$$

but because of the $100 ITC the investment generates a net tax saving. It was correct to use 34 percent as the tax rate in computing the cash flows even though the $100 ITC reduces all taxes that otherwise would be paid by the firm by $100 - 20.61 = $79.39. The average tax rate is not useful for decisions.

The interest rate used for time discounting should be on an after-tax basis. Currently only debt creates a tax shield, so the cost of debt should be multiplied by $(1 - t)$ to figure it on an after-tax basis. If the marginal tax rate is expected to change, then the expected tax rate for each specific period should be used. Placing the interest expense on an after-tax basis takes into consideration the tax shield of interest; the investment cash flows should not also double-count the interest tax deduction.

The Audit

With a free-standing investment, it is feasible to audit the operating results and compare the actual numbers with the projections that were used to justify the investment. When an investment is part of a more comprehensive project, it is frequently difficult or impossible to identify the benefits of a specific investment. If a new piece of equipment, for example, is expected to be able to improve productivity compared to the present equipment, after replacement the present equipment will be gone and the comparison of actual results will not be feasible.

One of the difficulties of using the capital budget postaudit was well expressed by a manager of capital budgeting who stated that "frequently the person who submitted the proposal is long since gone to another job." Despite the difficulties, investments should be subject to audit. The first stage of the audit should be the amount expended and the time taken in the construction process. The second stage of the audit should be to compare the operating results with the cash flows that were used to evaluate the project. One of the more important uses of the investment audit is to identify any systematic bias that is entering the cash flow projections. Bias may come from a division (the division always overestimates the benefits and underestimates the project cost) or can originate in a functional area (marketing tends to be optimistic in their forecasts). It is important for managers to know that their forecasts will be used not only for project evaluation, but also as a comparison with the actual observable results.

Capital Budgeting and Inflation

How do expectations of inflation affect investment decisionmaking? Inflation is rampant in a large percentage of the world's countries. While it is defined to be under control in the United States when it is less than 6 percent, an inflation rate of 6 percent is too large to be neglected in any capital budgeting analysis.

Managers tend to use a wide range of procedures to include inflation in the capital budgeting analysis. Basically there are two primary problems requiring solution: the adjustment of the cash flows and the choice of the rate of discount. A third problem dealing with tax depreciation is part of the cash flow adjustment problem.

Cash Flow with Inflation

There are two correct ways of factoring inflation into the capital budgeting analysis. One is to use nominal cash flows and the second is to use real cash flows. If the analysis is done correctly, it does not make a difference as to which method is used, but most firms use nominal cash flows.

Assume that the following set of cash flows is forecast for an investment opportunity:

Time	Cash Flow with Zero Inflation
0	−$2,000
1	+1,200
2	+1,100

Before using these cash flows we need to know the inflation assumption that was used in the forecast. The cash flows shown are based on a zero inflation rate, but assume that the forecast inflation rate for the next two years is 6 percent. If the forecast cash flows are perfectly correlated with inflation (a 6 percent inflation rate leads to a 6 percent increase in the cash flows), then the nominal cash flows for a 6 percent inflation rate will be

Time	Zero Inflation Cash Flow	Nominal Cash Flow	Inflation Factor
0	−$2,000	−$2,000.00	$(1.06)^0$
1	1,200	1,272.00	$(1.06)^1$
2	1,100	1,235.96	$(1.06)^2$

The internal rate of return using the real cash flows is 10 percent. The internal rate of return using the nominal cash flows is 16.6 percent.

If we deflate the nominal cash flows for inflation we will obtain the following "real" cash flows:

$$\frac{\$1,272}{1.06} = \$1,200,$$

$$\frac{\$1,235.96}{1.06^2} = \$1,100,$$

which are the same cash flows we started with before adjusting for inflation.

We can either start with real cash flows and adjust them for inflation to obtain nominal cash flows, or we can work with the real cash flows. Another alternative is to start with the nominal cash flows given 6 percent inflation and use the nominal flows; or to deflate them for inflation to obtain the real cash flows.

In the preceding example, the nominal cash flows were perfectly correlated with inflation. Now assume that with zero inflation we expect the same set of cash flows as before, but with 6 percent inflation the cash flows will be unaffected by the inflation (for example, they could be the cash flows from a two-year lease). We now have

Time	Cash Flow with Zero Inflation	Cash Flow with 6% Inflation	Real Cash Flow Given 6% Inflation
0	−$2,000	−$2,000	−$2,000.00
1	1,200	1,200	1,132.08
2	1,100	1,100	979.00

Now the real cash flows with inflation are different from the real and nominal cash flows with zero inflation. In fact, the real cash flows are decreased by the existence of inflation. This situation is similar to what happens when inflation erodes the value of depreciation tax deductions.

The nominal cash flows that are used for the project should reflect the prices of the inputs and the outputs of the project, given the forecast inflation rate. The decisionmaker needs the general level of inflation to determine the effect on the prices of the specific inputs and outputs, but it is these prices of specific inputs and outputs that are important. If with zero inflation an input costs $100, and if with 10 percent inflation the cost will be $106, then $106 is the relevant nominal cash flow, and $106/1.10 = $96.36 is the real cash flow. We can describe the cost in terms of the $96.36 real measure or in terms of the $106.00 nominal measure.

Tax Deductions

Nelson is one academic to consider the effect of inflation on investment decisions. Because tax depreciation deductions lose value with inflation, he found that, all other things equal, the "amount invested will typically be smaller the higher the rate of inflation."[1]

Kim came to a conclusion similar to Nelson's but allowed that inflation could cause income to change at a different rate from the rate of inflation; this adds another dimension to the analysis.[2] Inflation could have a favorable effect on income that might balance its unfavorable effect on tax depreciation deductions.

Managers should be aware that if a firm has depreciation tax deductions, the nominal cash flow changes probably will not be directly proportional to the changes in the price level. The example following is an illustration.

47

Assume that the corporate tax rate is 34 percent and straight-line depreciation is used. With zero inflation, we expect the following before- and after-tax cash flows to occur:

Time	Before-Tax Cash Flow	Depreciation	Taxable Income	Income Tax	After-Tax Cash Flow
0	−$2,000.00				
1	+1,303.03	$1,000	$303.03	$103.03	$1,200
2	+1,151.52	1,000	151.52	51.52	1,100

This is the same set of after-tax cash flows that we obtained previously with zero inflation and zero tax. Now assume that the before-tax nominal cash flows of time one and time two are both increased 6 percent by an annual 6 percent inflation rate:

$$\$1,303.03 \ (1.06) = \$1,381.21,$$
$$\$1,151.52 \ (1.06)^2 = \$1,293.85.$$

We now have

Time	Before-Tax Cash Flow	Depreciation	Taxable Income	Income Tax	After-Tax Cash Flow
0	−$2,000.00				
1	+1,381.21	$1,000	$381.21	$129.61	$1,251.60
2	+1,293.85	1,000	293.85	99.91	1,193.94

We can compare these after-tax cash flows with the nominal cash flows obtained when $1,200 and $1,100 were increased by 6 percent inflation per year.

Time	Cash Flow without Inflation with and without Taxes	Nominal Inflated After-Tax Cash Flow	Nominal Cash Flow (No Taxes) 6% Inflation
1	$1,200	$1,251.60	$1,272.00
2	1,100	1,193.94	1,235.96

The presence of inflation combined with the tax law convention that uses original cost depreciation deductions (unadjusted for inflation) means that the after-tax cash flows do not increase at the same rate as inflation:

$$\$1,200 \times 1.06 = \$1,272,$$
$$\$1,100 \times (1.06)^2 = \$1,235.96.$$

The value of the depreciation deductions decreases as the inflation rate increases. With zero inflation, the nominal and real value of the depreciation deductions would be $340 for each year. With 6 percent inflation per year the real value is

Period	Depreciation	Nominal Value of Tax Savings	Real Value of Tax Savings with Zero Inflation	Price Level Factor	Real Value of Tax Savings with 6% Inflation
1	$1,000	$340	$340	1.06^{-1}	$320.75
2	1,000	340	340	1.06^{-2}	$302.60

With inflation the real value of the depreciation deductions is eroded rapidly.

The Rate of Discount with Inflation

As capital budgeting decisions can be made using either a nominal or real interest rate, we need to distinguish between nominal and real rates. The nominal interest rate is the rate that is observed in the capital market. The real interest rate is equal to the nominal interest rate adjusted for inflation. We can link nominal and real rates as follows:

If k = nominal interest rate, r = real interest rate, and j = inflation rate, then

$$1 + r = \frac{1 + k}{1 + j}$$

and

$$k = r + j + rj.$$

For example, if $r = 0.10$ and $j = 0.06$, to earn a 10 percent real return an investor would have to earn a nominal return of 16.6 percent:

$$k = r + j + rj = 0.10 + 0.06 + 0.006 = 0.166.$$

With no inflation, an investment of $100 earning cash flows of $106 at time one would earn a real return of 6 percent. With 6 percent inflation, an investment of $100 earning cash flows of $116.60 would earn a 16.6 percent nominal return. The $116.60 of nominal cash flows translates to $116.60/1.06 = $110 real dollars. Thus the investor earning 16.6 percent nominal with 6 percent inflation earns a real return of 10 percent.

Consider the situation where with 6 percent inflation the projected nominal and real cash flows are

Time	Nominal Cash Flow	Real Cash Flow
0	$-$2,000.00	$-$2,000
1	1,272.00	1,200
2	1,235.96	1,100

This investment has a nominal internal rate of return of 16.6 percent. The real internal rate of return is 10 percent. This leads to an important conclusion. If nominal cash flows are used, a nominal discount rate must be used. If real cash flows are used, a real discount rate must be used. A major error made by managers is to discount real cash flows using the nominal interest rate. This procedure creates a bias against otherwise desirable investments.

Now let us assume that with a 6 percent inflation rate the observed (nominal) market interest rate is 11.3 percent. Solving for the implied real interest rate of r:

$$r = \frac{k - j}{1 + j} = \frac{0.113 - 0.06}{1.06} = 0.05.$$

The net present value of the investment using the nominal cash flows and the nominal interest rate of 11.3 percent is

$$NPV = -2,000 + \frac{1,272}{1.113} + \frac{1,235.96}{(1.113)^2} = \$140.59.$$

The net present value of the investment using the real cash flows and the real interest rate of 5 percent is

$$NPV = -2,000 + \frac{1,200}{1.05} + \frac{1,100}{(1.05)^2} = \$140.59.$$

We obtain exactly the same net present value using nominal cash flow and the nominal interest rate as we do using the real cash flows and the real discount rate. This equality will always hold.

Rappaport and Taggart conclude that while both the nominal and real approaches to capital budgeting under inflation are theoretically acceptable, the nominal cash flow approach is superior for two reasons. "First, corporate planning systems are invariably expressed in nominal rather than real terms, and, second, the nominal approach requires a market-based discount rate and thereby allows the incorporation of market inflation forecasts."[3] The second reason is less valid if the real interest rate is computed using the relationship $r = (k - j)/(1 + j)$ because this calculation includes both the market interest rate and the inflation forecast used in the cash flow calculation.

Cooley, Roenfeldt, and Chew extend the basic inflation analysis by including the fact that inflation is uncertain and that there is business risk.[4] Bailey and Jensen focus on situations where general price level changes affect the choice of mutually exclusive investments.[5] Mehta, Curley, and Fung investigate the impact of uneven inflation on the discount rate and conclude that "the nominal method is more expedient than the real method for implementation purposes."[6]

The Discount Rate and Taxes

We still have to consider income taxes in computing the discount rate. Assume there is one tax rate, t:

$$(1 - t)k = (1 - t)r + j + (1 - t)rj,$$

or

$$k = r + \frac{j}{1 - t} + rj.$$

In this formulation, k is the before-tax market return one has to earn in order to have a real return of r (before the income tax) and $(1 - t)r$ after tax.

Continuing the example, where $r = 0.10$ and $j = 0.06$, with $t = 0.34$, we would then have

$$k = 0.10 + \frac{0.06}{1 - 0.34} + 0.006,$$

$$= 0.10 + 0.091 + 0.006 = 0.197.$$

If with zero inflation, an investment of $100 earns 10 percent before tax, it will earn 6.6 percent after tax. Now let us assume a 6 percent inflation rate where the investor's objective is a 0.10 $(1 - 0.34) = 0.066$ real return after tax. If an investment of $100 earn 19.7 percent before tax or $119.70 before tax at time one, it will earn a 6.6 percent real after-tax return with 6 percent inflation.

Before-tax proceeds	$119.70
Less: Investment	100.00
Taxable income	19.70
Tax rate	×.34
Tax	6.70

Cash flow $= 119.70 - 6.70 = 113.00$

Real cash flow $= \dfrac{113.00}{1.06} = 106.60$

The before-tax proceeds of $119.70 lead to a 6.6 percent real return on the $100 initial investment. To earn a 6.6 percent real after-tax return with 6 percent inflation, it was necessary to earn 19.7 percent before tax. Because current tax laws offer little or no protection against inflation, the necessary nominal return increases rapidly as the inflation rate increases.

Gandolfi simplifies the relationship of the nominal and real rates somewhat but arrives at a similar conclusion.[7] In addition, he considers the effect on investment of having a capital gains tax. Ezzell and Kelly use an analysis similar to that followed above but recognize that a mixture of debt and common stock will be used by corporations and that the tax effects are more complex than we assume in this chapter.[8]

Inflation adds a layer of complexity to capital budgeting. There is no question that it is necessary to forecast the annual inflation rates for each year for the period of time that the asset being considered will operate so that the asset's input and output prices may be estimated. This is a difficult but important task.

Fortunately, once this information is obtained, the mechanics of computing the net present value are not complex. A firm can use nominal cash flows obtained using the price level forecasts discounted at the nominal (observed market rate) discount rates. A less widely used method is to project real cash flows obtained by adjusting the nominal cash flows for general price level changes and discount the real cash flows using a real interest rate obtained using the nominal rate and the general price level inflation rate. Both the real and nominal calculations will give the same net present value.

Conclusions

The estimation of cash flows is a difficult exercise for a person preparing a capital budgeting request, for it requires a large number of assumptions about the future. It is not difficult to offer a theoretically correct definition of cash flows, but in practice it is difficult to determine the cash flows for each year of an asset with a life of thirty years. If a paper company plants a tree today, at what price will it sell that tree (or the paper made from it) in thirty years?

A major error that is made under inflationary conditions is to discount real cash flows using a nominal discount rate. This error should be avoided. It adjusts for inflation twice.

As one survey respondent observed, "Focusing on the *relevant* costs for investment analysis: good cost accounting sometimes gets in the way of focusing on differential future costs for economic evaluations. This is an ongoing educational requirement."

For additional references on estimating cash flows for investment analysis; see notes 9–13.

4

Capital Budgeting
and Capital Rationing

*Most firms find, I think, that allocation of scarce
capital funds is the most difficult problem they face.*
An Assistant Controller

It is rare to talk to a group of managers concerning capital
budgeting without someone raising the issue of capital rationing.
What does a firm do if it does not have the capital to finance all
investments with a positive net present value?

Weingartner did an excellent job of summarizing the published literature on capital rationing. He properly defines two types
of capital rationing. There are both self-imposed expenditure limits
(possibly for purposes of maintaining control) and external expenditure limits imposed on the firm, as when banks are "loaned up."
He concludes that "the interpretation of capital rationing as a
market phenomenon is inconsistent with its internal assumptions
and its consequences are at variance with observation."[1] The usual
response by an academic to a manager's description of capital
rationing is to recommend raising more capital (possibly at a high
cost, which would reduce the number of eligible projects).

Capital Rationing

An Easy Solution

One easy solution is to define away the problem. Step 1 is to eliminate self-imposed limitations and raise the necessary capital so that all desirable investments can be accepted. Step 2 is to recognize that even where bank loans cannot be obtained, long-term debt or equity capital can be, so really there are no external limits.

It is true that there may be dilution of ownership, or that the capital may have an extremely high cost, but the capital can be obtained. This solution is not acceptable to operating managers who have to prepare the capital budget and who believe that they are limited in the capital they can spend. Frequently, managers believe that it is a bad time to raise new capital. They think the issue of stock or debt will adversely affect present investors in the firm, because the investment community does not know how good the firm's investment opportunities are. The asymmetry of information can arise when management knows things about its future prospects but the market does not have the same information. Competitive considerations may make it impossible to release enough information for the market value of the firm to increase sufficiently to justify a new issue.

Thus, while it is possible that capital could be obtained in the market, the capital constraint is binding for operating managers. Academics may argue that capital rationing can always be eliminated by going to the market, but the fact is that managers wish to rank independent investments so that they can choose the optimum subset given a total capital constraint.

Problems with Ranking

The task of explaining capital rationing becomes somewhat easier if it is recognized that there is no single measure of investment value that allows us to rank investments exactly. We cannot easily and exactly solve the problem that managers want us to solve.

Consider three investments with the following net present values:

Investment	Net Present Value	Ranking
A	$10,000,000	1
B	6,000,000	2
C	5,000,000	3

Using the net present value measures, investment A is ranked 1, but if B plus C did not have a larger initial outlay than A, the B plus C combination is better than A. Choosing A rather than B plus C would be in error, for B plus C has a net present value of $11 million, which is larger than A's $10 million.

The use of the internal rate of return method to rank independent investments also can be misleading. Assume the firm can finance either investment X or Y but not both. Investment Y will pay $19 a period for three years and an additional $100 at time three. After period one the firm can invest and borrow at an annual rate of 10 percent.

Investment	0	1	2	3	Internal Rate of Return
X	-100	132			0.32
Y	-100	19	19	119	0.19

Using the internal rates of return, X is preferred to Y, but using a 10 percent opportunity cost (the lending and borrowing rate) we have

	Net Present Value (0.10)
X	$20.00
Y	$22.38

and Y is better than X. The same conclustion can be reached by computing the amount of cash one would have with each of the two investments at time three: $159.72 of cash with investment

X and $162.89 with Y (excluding the $100 outlay). Including the outlay there would be $26.62 with X and $29.79 with Y at time three.

This example illustrates the theoretical difficulty of using the internal rate of return to rank investments. However, let us consider what happens if X is accepted because of its ranking (a higher IRR). That is, a net present value of $20.00 is accepted rather than $22.38. If an investment with a positive net present value can be found at time one to replace X (it can be a second investment X), then the net present value gap between investments X and Y can be closed; in fact, X can beat Y. The reinvestment assumption becomes important in evaluating the investments to be accepted in a capital rationing situation.

Another popular method of evaluating investments is to compute the profitability index (sometimes called the index of present value) where

$$Profitability\ index = \frac{Present\ value\ of\ benefits}{Present\ value\ of\ outlays}$$

With X and Y we would have

Profitability Index
$X \quad \dfrac{120}{100} = 1.2$
$Y \quad \dfrac{122.38}{100} = 1.2238$

and this ranking accords with the previous conclusion that Y is better than X. We will now assume the firm can invest $200 and that a third investment Z costing $200 at time zero and time one will have the following cash flows:

0	1	Net Present Value (0.10)
−$200	+$490.60 −220.00	$46

The $220 outlay at time one can be the reclaiming of a coal field or the dismantling of a nuclear energy plant.

The profitability index of Z is 446/400 = 1.115, so X and Y are both better than Z. But Z with a net present value of $46 is better than X plus Y. If the net cash flow of $270.60 for period one is used, the profitability index is 246/200 = 1.23. The value of the profitability index depends on the method of calculation.

The three methods of ranking independent investments that we have illustrated all are deficient. A fourth method of coping with capital rationing is to prepare a linear programming solution.[2] This approach, pioneered by Weingartner, offers an elegant solution. There are, however, two major problems. First, it still is necessary to make an assumption about the discount rate to be used to obtain a net present value that is to be maximized. There is not general agreement about the discount rate to be used. Second, any realistic formulation for a large corporation will be costly. It will be costly to obtain the data and costly to obtain a solution, because the data requirements are very large. It is necessary to project cash flows not only for the investments to be made immediately, but also for investments to be made in future time periods. Management is not likely to have a great deal of confidence in recommendations flowing from a complex mathematical model that requires so much information.

Several Feasible Solutions

Interestingly, the same complexity of uncertainty that led to frustrating conclusions in the discount rate discussion leads to a pragmatic solution to the capital rationing problem. Let us assume there are $400 million of acceptable investment opportunities competing for $100 million of available capital. This is a capital rationing situation. It is important to remember that the cash flows of most (if not all) of the $400 million investments found to be acceptable are uncertain. Management will have preferences for some of the investments because of the risk characteristics or because of overall strategy considerations. Management can use a combination of quantitative measures and subjective evaluation techniques to choose the best way of spending the $100 million among the $400 million of acceptable alternatives.

If objective rankings are desired, investments can be ranked using the internal rate of return of each investment. These rankings then can be adjusted for risk considerations (the risk premium offered by the investment in excess of the default-free lending rate can be compared to the riskiness of the investment).

Alternatively, the net present value of all feasible sets of investments (given the limit on capital spending) can be computed. The set with the largest net present value can be acccepted even though the rejection of other acceptable investments implies that a larger discount rate should be used (the opportunity cost for capital is larger than the discount rate).

The Rate of Discount

Capital rationing complicates the already difficult task of determining the rate of discount (the required return). Baumol and Quandt argue persuasively that the stockholder's consumption time preferences determine the optimal set of investments.[3] Bacon writes that it should be the firm's opportunity cost. He states, for example, "in capital rationing situations, however, the decision-maker must develop a discount (reinvestment) rate based upon internal investment situations."[4] Weingartner concludes "there is nothing in the present analysis which would bring into question the appropriateness of using the cost of capital as the discount rate when firms limit capital expenditures voluntarily."[5]

Weingartner recognizes that the use of the cost of capital neglects the cost of lost opportunities and concludes: "Where such opportunity losses are more than compensated for in the form of better planning and control is an issue which requires further study."[6]

There is no shortage of complex mathematical solutions. For example, Thompson ties together the capital asset pricing model with mathematical programming to solve a single-period problem. He concludes: "Developing a multi-period approach to capital budgeting using a multi-period capital asset pricing model appears more formidable."[7] Rychel, on the other hand, offers a mixed-integer linear programming solution for capital rationing that was actually used at the Cities Service Company. He summarizes the benefits of the process: "The capital budgeting model helps management allocate the company's discretionary funds in a manner most beneficial to the company and its shareholders.... . It determines capital requirements and dividend capabilities over the planning horizon."[8] The model defines capital investment, dividends, return on assets, and so on, for the next twenty years. The information requirements are immense, and it is unlikely that the academic community would agree with the objective function (it includes "maximize ROA" and "maximize net income growth"). It is easy to have very sophisticated mathematical tools solving the incorrect problem.

Conclusions

In solving capital rationing problems there is room for judgment. It is important that managers understand the limitations of mathematical models. If restraints are placed on spending capital so that it is necessary to reject some otherwise acceptable investments, it will not be feasible to find a theoretically correct mathematical model for making investment decisions unless a mathematical programming technique is used, and one is willing to accept an assumption concerning the appropriate discount rate. One can use the internal rate of return or profitability indexes as if they give good reliable rankings, but a purist will object.

If after evaluating investment, taking both time value and risk into consideration, there are still too many investments for the given amount of capital, there are three sensible solutions in addition to the mathematical programming solution. The first solution (popular among academics) is to raise more capital. If the investments are truly desirable, capital should be available in the market. The second solution is to invoke strategy considerations and then see if there is still a surplus of investment opportunities. The third solution is to recognize that the projects have all survived the evaluation process and that they all promise to increase the stockholders' well-being. While a theoretical purist properly will object to a ranking of independent investments using their internal rate of return measures, given the uncertainty that exists in estimating cash flows, such a ranking combined with risk evaluations can be used to facilitate capital rationing. If the forecasts are valid, good investments are being accepted.

While marginally better investments could conceivably have been chosen, when we allow uncertainty to enter, it is clear the search for the exactly correct set of investments can be adequately satisfied by the approximate discounted cash flow measures.

A survey respondent asks, "Why do the business units still feel there is a shortage of funds when the corporate perception is a lack of projects?" See notes 9–21 for more references on capital rationing.

5

Capital Budgeting and Corporate Strategy

Our experience is that the business groups always request more budgeted funds than are available. As a result, our instructions call for a ranking of the capital projects. Even with this ranking, it is difficult to arrive at the final capital budget.
Corporate Vice President,
Financial Planning

With certainty we can supply exact decision rules for choosing among investment alternatives. When uncertainty is introduced, and in the presence of capital rationing, there are valid disagreements on exactly how decisions should be made. We know how to avoid some errors, but we are less successful in supplying easily applied decision rules for making theoretically correct capital budgeting decisions. Why do firms use methods that are obviously inferior from a theoretical viewpoint? We shall see there are several explanations.

Financial Planning

The search for ways of coping with massive data and uncertainty has resulted in a wide range of financial planning techniques using quantitative modeling. Among the authors offering such models are Carleton,[1] Elliot,[2] Francis and Rowell,[3] Gershefski,[4] Myers and Pogue,[5] Warren and Shelton,[6] and Weingartner.[7]

This attempt to achieve exactness with its inevitable addition of complexity has led to something of a backlash, with authors arguing that some of the less complex inexact tools serve useful functions. For example, Weingartner explains how the payback period calculation, an imprecise method that leaves out much useful information, is helpful nevertheless in a world of uncertainty.[8] It supplies information that other calculations omit by telling us the length of time needed to break even. It also serves to help prevent biasing the net present value and internal rate of return methods by loading the benefits of the later years (thus leading to acceptance but delaying the evaluation of whether the project was successful).

Fogler, in a paper titled "Overkill in Capital Budgeting Technique?", writes that "certain aspects of the funds rationing problem ensure that in many instances selection by simple ranking will approximate closely the solution reached by more expensive and cumbersome mathematical programming."[9] He hedges his position by then defining situations where mathematical programming models are useful.

In 1974 K. Larry Hastie published his classic paper, "One Businessman's View of Capital Budgeting." His position is that firms should avoid excessively complex measurement techniques. He states "Investment decision making could be improved significantly if the emphasis were placed on asking the appropriate strategic questions and providing better assumptions rather then on increasing the sophistication of measurement techniques.[10]

Consider the Fortune 500 firm that did an incomplete study of an industry, projecting sales of $50 million in the first year it entered the industry. This estimate was the cornerstone on which the investment analysis was based. The analysis, however, failed to consider the actions of competitors and the distribution complexities of the product line. Actual sales were $5 million for the first year. Competitors reacted vigorously to the entry of the new product line with the result that actual sales were 10 percent of projected sales. The company lost $30 million in a year when it expected a profit from the project.

. Hastie's position is not that inferior evaluation techniques should be used, but rather that the "use of incorrect assumptions has been a more significant source of bad investment decisions than has the use of simple measurement techniques."[11]

Pinches accepts Hastie's observations, as well as those of others of a similar viewpoint, and reinforces their criticisms. He states that "by focusing on these narrowly defined problems, both academicians and practitioners have consequently devoted little attention to the overall strategic question of how effectively capital budgeting interfaces with the actual resource allocation process employed in practice. Our major problem is not the lack of knowledge of specific details related to the techniques as they presently exist; rather, it is the myopic or shortsighted view of capital budgeting held in both the business and academic communities."[12]

In this chapter we want to consider a strategy approach to allocating investment funds. The conclusions are consistant with those of Bierman.[13]

The Other Extreme
To this point our recommendation has been for a firm to accept all independent investments with a positive net present value (risk-adjusted), or, equivalently, accept all independent investments that have an internal rate of return greater than the appropriate required return. If this is not possible because of internal capital rationing, managers can follow either a programming approach or the inexact but approximately correct methods such as profitability index or internal rate of return to rank investments. The rankings are not exactly correct, but evidence and logic indicate they will not be far from the theoretically correct solution.

There is another school of thought that recommends basing resource allocations on corporate strategy considerations organized in some systematic way. One method that has been implemented is to use a two-by-two classification scheme as shown in figure 5–1 (the classification schemes also have expanded to three-by-three and four-by-four tables).

Figure 5–1. Relative Market Share

Market **Growth** **Rate**		Strong	Weak
	High	Stars	Question Marks
	Low	Cash Cows	Dogs

The two-by-two scheme shows the Boston Consulting Group (BCG) classic labels for each of the four boxes. Each distinctive business unit activity of the firm should fall in one of these boxes.

An extension of the BCG analysis used by many firms is to specify different required returns (hurdle rates) for each box. For example, in the case of low market growth and weak market share (a dog), a firm might impose the following rules:

◆ Expansion investments—none allowed
◆ Labor efficiency—a minimum 40 percent internal rate of return
◆ Energy efficiency—a minimum 30 percent internal rate of return

An investment for a "star" activity, on the other hand, might have to earn only 12 percent to be acceptable. Implicitly, these arbitrary strategic rules are saying that the cash flow analyses prepared by the divisions are not to be believed.

Assume a firm normally requires a return of 12 percent. If a "dog" presented an expansion plan that earned 40 percent, either the errors in the presentation should be identified, or the plan should be accepted. If a dog can earn 15 percent with increased labor efficiency and the firm requires 12 percent, then either the faults in the calculations should be identified, or the investment accepted.

No matter how finely the martix is subdivided, management cannot depend for decisionmaking judgments on a classification scheme. It is a very unreliable method of allocating resources. But, this does not mean strategy does not have a place in resource allocation. Management might decide that the future of the corporation is best served by investing in retailing rather than oil exploration. This is a strategic decision, and investment spending choices should be consistent with it.

A decision to spend on retailing rather than on oil exploration should be based on analysis and judgment, not on whether one of the activities today is a dog and the other a star. Each corporation has skills and knowledge that it should exploit. Today's dog might be tomorrow's star if the right personnel and ideas are present and the correct investments are made. The merit of each investment should be evaluated using as good concrete evidence (calculations) as feasibly can be obtained.

A Compromise

We have now considered the two extremes. One method uses only economic measures of value to evaluate investment alternatives. The other procedure concludes that with uncertainty the economic measures cannot be trusted and that it is necessary to allocate resources based on the overall corporate strategy.

Now we will consider a three-level method of making investment decisions:

Level 1: Allocation based on the economic measures (net present value and internal rate of return) for low-risk investments

Level 2: Allocation based on the past performance of the divisions

Level 3: Allocation based on the strategic plan approved by top management

Level One

It is sound to use discounted cash flow measures when the risk level is low. This would mean that funds could be spent on dogs, as long as the expected return were high enough. This, of course, assumes that it is expected that the dog will not be divested, and that the cash flows are accepted as reliable estimates.

Level Two

Allocations would be based on past performance. Assume the following facts apply where $80 million is to be allocated using past performance.

Division	Income before Interest	Interest on Capital Used	Income after Interest	Percentage
A	$70,000,000	$10,000,000	$ 60,000,000	0.6
B	60,000,000	20,000,000	40,000,000	0.4
C	10,000,000	10,000,000	0	
		Total	$100,000,000	1.0

The allocation would be

80,000,000 × 0.6 = 48,000,000 for Division A.
80,000,000 × 0.4 = 32,000,000 for Division B.

Such an allocation would reward divisions for earning income above the firm's required return on its captial.

The interest deduction for each division is equal to the division's capital times the firm's capital cost. For the example, if the interest rate used is 10 percent, we have

Division	Capital Used	Interest Rate	Interest Cost
A	$100,000,000	0.10	$10,000,000
B	200,000,000	0.10	20,000,000
C	100,000,000	0.10	10,000,000
			$40,000,000

If a division cannot earn the 10 percent required return on new investments, it would do better to return the capital to the firm than to invest it in undesirable projects.

Level Three

Allocations to the three divisions would depend on the long-run objectives of the firm and subjective strategy considerations.

The size of the level one allocations would depend on the number of safe investments, but given that the definition of "safe" is subjective, even the level one allocations are subjective. Thus the net result would be a subjective allocation based on the three types of allocation. If the firm has a capital budget of $200 million, it would have to decide how much is to be allocated based on discounted cash flow measures, how much allocated to divisions based on past performance (and then invested based on discounted cash flow), and how much allocated based on strategy considerations (and any other factors that top management wants to consider).

Finance theory does not accept that past performance affects investment allocation. Investment allocation should be based on the forecasts, but there are two reasons for using past performance. First, it is relatively objective; it is thus likely to be accepted by managers as being a fairer method of allocation than simply giving the investment funds to those divisions that are most optimistic. Second, the evidence of actual performance results may temper possible excessive optimism. If the forecasts used in investment analysis were unbiased forecasts, there would by no need to use past performance results in the allocation process.

Competition

Competitive considerations must include actions of the firm making the decision, as well as those of competing firms. Often management fails to consider the effect of its own plans on the market price of the product being produced and the factors of production being used. A major paper company will double its paper-making capacity without ever considering the effect that the increased capacity it is supplying will have on paper prices.

Another consideration, of course, is the action of competitors. If the object of building a new paper plant is to increase share of market, a competitor might react by also building capacity so that it can increase its share of the market. The result of such an action and counteraction can be excess capacity and reduction in profits for the entire industry. a firm has to consider the effect of its actions on the markets in which it operates as well as how its decisions are likely to affect the decisions of its competitors. Techniques for analyzing industries and competitors have been well described by Porter.[14]

Strategy

Strategy should be considered in evaluating investments. Assume the management of a firm accepts the investment analysis that leads to an accept decision, yet rejects the investment. The rejection can be because of strategy considerations. An oil company, for instance, may decide it does not want to invest in mining operations or retailing. Implicit in these decisions might be a conclusion that, given a lack of expertise, the cash flows are not to be believed. Top management cannot evaluate the information that is presented to it, thus rejects the investments.

It is also possible for a firm to accept an investment for strategy reasons even though the net present value is negative. But here, the reason for acceptance must be that top management forecasts future benefits arising from the investment that are not captured in the cash flow analysis.

Strategy considerations are important, but they should be consistent with good discounted cash flow analysis. There does not need to be any inconsistency between good DCF calculations and decisions based on strategy considerations. Decisions should be consistent if the investment analysis is done correctly and completely. If some of the uncertainty considerations are difficult to quantify, numerical analysis can be supplemented by strategy considerations.

The mutually exclusive investement decision is one example of a decision where the input numbers are reliable normally, and where investment calculations are an important guide for making the decision. In making mutually exclusive investment decisions it is important that the alternatives be compared using correct investment evaluation techniques (net present value is the easiest method to use). The decision to enter the automobile industry is a strategy decision; any cash flow analysis is subordinate to the strategy decision to enter or not enter the industry. But once it has been decided to enter the industry, there should be good capital budgeting analyses using net present value to base further decisions on size of plant and type of equipment.

Some Observations from the Survey

Many of the firms indicated that strategy considerations affected the choice of investments. Among the interesting observations were the following:

> The problem has evolved a bit further: allocation of capital by type of project (maintenance, saving, expansion or new ventures) vs. strategy for the business segment involved, vs. relative size of the investment. What emerges is a complex three/dimensional matrix involving a whole series of threshold rates.
>
> *An Assistant Controller, Planning*

> The aggregate of these submittals is reviewed at the corporate level for its impact on earnings and cash flow, as well as for the strategic desirability of proceeding with major programs. It is typical during this review process that some projects are deleted, deferred, or reduced in scope, while a few other programs are accelerated or increased in scope. Ultimately, the program is endorsed by our Executive Committee and Board of Directors.
>
> *Manager, Corporate Planning*

> As evidenced by the recent turmoil in energy markets, our ability to forecast the future is imprecise at best. We therefore take into consideration the historical performance of the divisions when allocating capital. Because the results of discounted cash flow calculations are only as good as today's assumptions, blind use of this methodology would be unwise. For example, too often these analyses do not adequately anticipate the actions of our competitors, which may reduce the benefits we might otherwise expect. Thus there always is a place for "gut instinct" or old fashioned experience—call it what you will—in the capital budgeting process.
>
> *Manager, Corporate Planning*

The imprecise nature of the capital budgeting process is made clear by the responses. Given such imprecision, managers are reluctant to put too much faith in any methodology that—at least in some sense—is more precise than the inputs.

Options and Valuing Flexibility

The next academic thrust in capital budgeting is in the application of option thinking to the evaluation of investment alternatives (see Mason and Merton[15] and Trigeorgis and Mason.[16])

This development has two major branches. One approach attempts to apply modern option theory including an extension of the Black-Scholes mathematical model.[17] The second approach uses the essential concepts of option theory but employs a basic decision tree (or expected value) method of analysis.

Option theory is useful in placing a value on flexibility. Flexibility includes the timing of the initiation and completion of a project, the choice of the best of a set of mutually exclusive investments, and the opportunity to extend the investment on the completion of the investment's normal life. The value of flexibility can be estimated using the theory of pricing options, but frequently this valuation will be extremely complex, and it will be necessary to substitute a qualitative input. We do not yet know how to apply the mathematical option model in a manner that will be simply understood.

There is little question that the applicaiton of option theory to capital budgeting decisions is potentially a major capital budgeting development and we can expect to see many academic papers dealing with the application of the option concepts to real investments to be made by corporations. Useful insights can be gained now from the basic concepts.

However, it will be some time before the mathematical models of option theory are widely used in industry. But, even where exact quantitative results cannot be obtained, option theory will make an important contribution to improved investment decision making by calling attention to the existence of alternatives that introduce flexibility, and the need to value these investment alternatives.

Conclusions

The discounted cash flow measures should be the basis of any investment allocation plan. But given the fact that uncertainty exists, it is reasonable for management to evaluate the validity of DCF results and decide whether they should be superseded by more subjective evaluations. Judgement cannot be replaced by a slavish obedience to quantitative measures that are based on very unreliable estimates of cash flows. On the other hand, once the cash flows of each period are estimated, they should be discounted back to the present using as sound computational procedures as are available.

When future generations of managers evaluate investments, they will have the same types of concerns as the managers of today. Moreover, we can be sure they will discount for time using a present value calculation; in addition, they will make some type of risk adjustment. There is no reason for not taking advantage of these calculations in a sensible fashion today. Both net present value and internal rate of return are extremely useful techniques that should be used by all business firms.

It is true that if they are used badly, these tools will adversely affect the quality of the decisionmaking. For example, if the required hurdle rate for a normal-risk investment is inflated to 40 percent in a year when the after-tax borrowing rate is 6 percent, it is unlikely that the discounted cash flow methods will lead to good decisions. If conventional accounting practices are used to project the first two years' incomes and ROIs, and these projections are allowed to influence the investment decision, it is likely that good investments will be rejected.

The conclusion is clear. Use the best DCF methods of evaluating investments. Use them with care, and use them to accomplish the objectives for which they are designed. Make sure the assumptions of the analysis are sensible.

A survey respondent comments "The most difficult aspect of capital budgeting is the process of relating the capital budget to the operating budget and the strategic plan. How do these three plans/budgets interrelate? If we provide more or less capital, what happens? In fact, all three plans/budgets are dynamic and changing thereby making the final budget/plan an imprecise thing at best."

Appendix

Executives Speak Out on Capital Budgeting Issues

Excerpts from Letters (1984–1985 Survey)

Accounting Effects

Economic returns (e.g., DCF) are given less weight than pro forma book income effects of capital projects.

Ideally, management operates a company for the long-term health of the enterprise and its shareholders. Practically, decisions are often made for short-term benefit. Through personal experience, we at [. . .] understand the threat of corporate raiders. We know that the only true defense is higher stock prices, and we know that higher stock prices come from higher earnings. We also realize that investors are impatient; they want high returns now. Adding to the problem is the fact that the financial analysts expect quarter-to-quarter earnings improvement—so does the board of directors. In fact, the board of directors sanctions and promotes incentive systems designed to reward short-term performance.

What does this mean to capital budgeting? Obviously, it could mean that capital investment decisions will be strongly biased toward those that produce short-term results.

A capital budgeting system should tie into the long-range planning process, rather than be just a system of accepting or rejecting individual projects. Also, the capital budgeting system should tie into a procedure for measurement of performance; that is, accountability should be an integral part of the system. But, most often management is more concerned with short-term results; therefore, accomplishing the above is difficult.

Finally, it is difficult to audit the actual rate of return of a productive asset for comparison to the assumed rate when the acquisition was approved.

Probably one of the greatest negative effects on capital budgeting techniques is management's response to short-term operating results.

Capital Rationing

We have attempted a variety of approaches for allocating the buget—various prioritizations, negative impact assessments on maintenance projects, comparative economic returns on profit adding projects, forced crossroughing between business units, and others. Overlaying these considerations is the broader issue of strategic direction of business units, and proper determination of the fit of proposed capital projects with that direction. The whole process is further complicated by the emotionalism of each business unit and plant wanting to protect its own interests, which at times are subjective and not compatible with overall corporate interests.

When the worldwide summary of estimated capital expenditures receives the agreement of top management, our system works well. However, when forecasted spending exceeds an acceptable level, implementing changes to the forecast from the "top down" is extremely difficult. Without obvious projects to eliminate, it is hard to cut spending in a manner that objectively eliminates the least economically justified items. Each division feels it has the highest priority activities requiring the dollars budgeted.

It often appears that management is not only concerned about impacts of spending on debt rating and near-term book income but also has an unusual degree of skepticism regarding the numerator of the project calculations. Rather than fighting through the assumptions in the numerator to discover the source of over-optimism, management tends to clamp on overall spending guidelines and strategy guidelines.

Cash Flow Calculation

Incomplete costs have been for many years the most common fault in the rationalization of a capital project proposal. This continues to be true. The errors of omission are also often difficult types to detect. The two general areas in which omissions occur are a) working capital requirements, and b) impact on general plant costs—infrastructure.

In considering the proposals of individual operating centers, it is difficult to determine the availability of underutilized assets in other operating centers that would fulfill the requirements of the requesting center.

Developing and implementing a system for economic evaluation and management authorization of capital projects has not been particularly difficult for us. Minor problems have been primarily associated with injudicious use of incremental investment in the economic evaluation, optimism in projecting project benefits, and maintenance of control to assure delegated approval authority is not violated and the approved project scope is not exceeded.

Hurdle Rates

Another observation relates to the use of hurdle rates. While hurdle rates may be useful when capital funds are limited and some form of rationing is required, I do not think they should be used as an absolute test (a "go" or "no go" decision tool). Too many variables and assumptions go into return on investment analysis for this. Just as a project that appears to exceed the hurdle rate can turn sour, so too can one that appears to fall below the rate become a significant future profit generator among a company's portfolio of businesses.

A company operating a porfolio of businesses, particularly major international operations, needs to ensure that its cost of capital-based hurdle rate properly reflects the finanical and business characteristics of the unit in which the proposed investment is being made.

Our operating companies do not universally agree on a methodology to arrive at their cost of capital and required rates of return for various capital projects. Because a corporate-developed cost of capital is not dictated to our operating companies, they must arrive at their own cost of capital. The operating companies must then adjust that cost of capital for project risk to arrive at a required rate of return for a given capital project.

In general, we feel that our capital budgeting process is effective and reasonably efficient. One area of confusion, however, is the whole issue of hurdle rates. Like most large companies, we arrive at this "threshold rate" by first estimating our weighted average cost of capital and then adjusting it upward to compensate for noneconomic projects.

Currently, we consider the riskiness of projects through a relatively high discount rate and an approval process that requires executive committee approval for projects over $5 million and board of directors' approval over $10 million. There is some sentiment in favor of different discount rates for different investment classes. However, it is my opinion that we are several steps away from effectively implementing risk-adjusted present value factors (RAPVFs). Risk preference and the time value of money seem, at times, inexorably linked.

Method of Evaluation

ROI is preferred to the NPV method, in general, because the time and effort associated with changing over to an NPV system outweigh the relatively minor additional benefits (most of which are theoretical) of an NPV system.

[. . .] uses several different financial measures in evaluating investment proposals including Internal Rate of Return (IRR), Discounted Payback, Profitability Index, and "Proof Year" Operating Return on Investment. The greatest weight is accorded to IRR in most cases; for simplicity, I will focus on this measure as though it were our sole criterion.

Textbook theory holds that a firm should undertake all projects that will provide an IRR in excess of the cost of capital. By definition, the financing costs for such projects should be less than their financial returns. The principal problem with this theory is that projected IRRs are not always realized, that is, projects that appear attractive on a forecast basis may fail to return the cost of capital.

Discounted cash flow analysis was seen to be biased against steel plant projects with long construction periods and long economic lives.

Our operating companies agree that a discounted cash flow framework is appropriate in evaluating capital projects. Our companies also believe assumptions are the driving force in most capital budgeting projects, which necessitates the need for sensitivity analysis on major assumptions.

[. . .] uses the MAPI method and/or DCF to financially justify capital expenditure projects. As both of these approaches have been in place for years, implementation is not a problem.

Optimism

Overly optimistic forecasting has been a continuing challenge in [. . .] capital budgeting and probably concerns many other companies. Various approaches are available to offset optimistic forecasting, none a panacea. Hurdle rates in excess of the cost of capital can be required for projects to leave a "margin for error"; unfortunately, this practice may encourage even more optimistic forecasting. Financial returns for approved projects can be monitored several years later versus the initial forecast. Although shortfalls on project returns cannot be rectified after the fact, the follow-up program may identify areas of potential improvement in project forecasting.

Marketing plans tend to "assume" the additional capacity will be sold; they tend to be optimistic, or they tend toward extrapolation of the trend line. The vital components essential to the successful execution of the market plan are often missing; therefore, it is difficult to judge its business validity.

The performance of the project after completion is never (almost) as good as promised in the approval document. This is probably the most significant problem in our capital budgeting process and one for which we have no viable solution. Post-audits have never done the job and imposed or self-imposed monitoring of key checkpoints has also not been entirely satisfactory.

We have an excellent record on projected capital costs, expense projections, labor productivity, etc. But when it comes to volume, market share and price projections, we tend to err on the optimistic side. A healthy internal rate of return can drop well below our cost of capital when the volume for a project doesn't materialize, or the marketplace restricts the projected price levels. A refined technique for quantitative analysis is little comfort when the base assumptions turn sour.

There is some institutional suspicion that project sponsors are overly optimistic concerning their project's potential benefits. The company has a relatively high hurdle rate, especially for new product ventures (30 percent). There may be a vicious circle where project sponsors overestimate benefits in order to meet the high hurdle rate, and the hurdle rate is kept high to discount over-estimated benefits. The audit or reconciliation of projected to actual benefits is limited. Once a project has been undertaken (especially a large one), there is a tendency to consider additional investments as requirements. Are sunk costs really sunk?

Organization

One difficulty is that all projects cannot be reviewed and weighed against one another at a single place and point in time. Instead, within an overall strategy, decisions on individual projects are reviewed one at a time.

Implementing capital budgeting techniques depends on judgement and foresight of those looking into the future. Sophisticated analysis seldom compensates for bad judgment.

The process of corporate people becoming "comfortable" with a project often takes time to get needed information not originally supplied by the business unit manager, who becomes impatient with and critical of the process in the meantime.

Although part of an approved strategy and included in an approved capital budget, individual projects require an inordinate amount of effort to secure approval. Problems with individual project justification (IRR), inflated capital estimates (as compared to forecast), arbitrary capital freezes imposed because of cash/profit problems, all cause delays in approval of individual projects.

As you know, business is moving at a faster and faster pace—the survivors react quickly. To take advantage of rapidly changing markets, capital equipment lead times and production crises, decisions often need to be made swiftly. Unfortunately, the corporate bureaucracy and the hierarchy gets in the way. Our investment analysis and approval process takes months to complete. Smart managers know they can't wait that long and they immediately jump at "once in a lifetime" opportunities. Sometimes our analysis is done quite a bit after the fact.

The continuous flows of project opportunities, deletions of opportunities, etc., make the usual model of having all the project data available at once for capital budgeting decisions quite unrealistic.

Conducting present value discounted cash flow analysis of ROIs among eight relatively independent operating companies presents problems of consistency in how the mechanics of the analysis is conducted. Periodically instructions have to be reissued to assure consistency.

Although our analytical staff is most competent, nonanalytical people, including upper management, do not have sufficient analytical understanding to permit the full bag of analytical tools to be used. As a result I feel we miss some investment opportunities.

I regard "paralysis by analysis" as the greatest problem in capital budgeting. A lot of business decisions, including sending money on capital projects, can be made quickly and without resorting to time-consuming and repetitive analysis. Our company, and I think most companies, would be better off if they could concentrate their analysis on the difficult problems and not waste so much time analyzing the obvious.

Qualitative Inputs

My intent was to convey that, while we do endeavor to analyze our capital decisions, the process is on of both analysis and subjective judgment. As you can imagine, experience is a key factor in our ability to make correct subjective judgments, and one message you may wish to convey is the importance of this element to any capital budgeting approach.

Obviously capital budgeting decisions cannot be based solely on the numbers. Even after satisfying oneself that the cash flows have been accounted for correctly, the final decisions still hinge on such intangibles as future manufacturing flexibilities, future labor availability, and customer service ability.

Capital budgeting techniques are applicable for too few projects. For many projects, a company can waste valuable effort trying to force fit data into an intuitively obvious decision. For example, a company's continued existence is placed in jeopardy if its effluent remains untreated. Should there be a major effort to ascribe a rate of return for a waste treatment plant?

The final analysis is highly influenced by the wisdom of the analyst and must be reviewed and "judged" by the appropriate level of management commensurate with the level of investment. It should also be recognized that there are always those capital items that are purchased irrespective of what the financial analysis shows. Investments determined to be required to protect our position in the marketplace of a particular product line or required to perform under a contract are examples that would fall in this category.

Risk

Our ability to forecast the future is imprecise at best. We therefore take into consideration the historical performance of the divisions when allocating capital. Because the results of discounted cash flow calculations are only as good as today's assumptions, blind use of this methodology would be unwise. For example, too often these analyses do not adequately anticipate the actions of our competitors, which may reduce the benefits we might otherwise expect. Thus there always is a place for "gut instinct" or old fashioned experience—call it what you will—in the capital budgeting process.

The economic value of capital projects that involve lead times of three to five years varies substantially with different price scenarios. Because the overall project economics are no more accurate than their least accurate component, the petroleum industry is routinely misled by the precision with which costs can be projected in contrast to revenues.

An ROI that depends heavily on incremental sales is viewed far more skeptically than one that derives its major cash flows from labor or material savings.

As the pace of business accelerates, inability to anticipate the capital requirements arising from new opportunities becomes more critical.

Extension of basic capital investment analysis to include more "sophisticated" techniques, such as risk analysis or divisional cost of capital concepts, has usually floundered, for such techniques have not enjoyed the support of operational management. Such extensions of the basic capital investment analysis are perceived as too much of a "numerical exercise" with limited additional utility to the decisionmaker. I should add that the [. . .] company is now very capital-intensive, and this lack of capital intensity undoubtedly shapes management's perceptions.

Strategy

In allocating capital, the divisions rely heavily on the discounted cash flow internal rate of return methodology. Strategic expansion, new products, and cost reduction projects that exceed a minimum hurdle rate (normally 12 to 20 percent) are added to a "good housekeeping" base and serve as the basis for divisional submittals. The aggregate of these submittals is reviewed at the corporate level for its impact on earnings and cash flow, as well as for the strategic desirability of proceeding with major programs. It is typical during this review process that some projects are deleted, deferred or reduced in scope, while a few other programs are accelerated or increased in scope. Ultimately, the program is endorsed by our executive committee and board of directors.

Any major capital project must pass two tests of strategic fit, that with the long-range plan of the business unit, and that with the overall corporate investment strategy.

There are certainly some very real situations in which a particular project does not look attractive in and of itself but yet is an integral part of an overall strategy which is highly desirable. Conversely, we have projects that by themselves are outstanding but are part of an overall business on the decline. For example, we have closed facilities that were only recently equipped with highly productive and highly effective pieces of machinery. The project justification looked outstanding!

Both DCF and sensitivity analysis, however, are employed in the decisionmaking process in the context of the strategies and grid positions of our strategic business units (SBUs). Thus a capital project is not considered solely on the basis of its DCF, but as part of an SBU's overall strategy, whether it be for growth, maintenance, or harvest of the business. This strategic approach to appropriating capital can result in different decisions than if classical capital allocation methods, such as selecting projects with the highest DCF, or those that exceed a given hurdle rate, are employed.

What we discovered was that we were doing most of the operational pieces of our capital management process relatively well, but we were not really connecting that work with a strategic plan that identified what we wanted to accomplish long term. By operational work, I mean the financial techniques (the NPV and IRR calculations to evaluate capital projects) and the project management and engineering skills necessary to prepare and submit capital requests. In essence, we were managing capital *projects* relatively effectively, but did not fully understand how our overall capital *program* was going to impact on our business results. What was missing was a strategic vision that could provide a context in which to make effective capital resource decisions.

Each year our twenty-six business units submit a list of capital projects for the following year. This list is not a completed request for approval to use funds, but rather a brief description of projects to be proposed. At the same time each business unit is submitting a profit plan for the next several years. Their profit plans are aggregated to become a projected balance sheet and income statement for the company as a whole. At this point, our chairman will determine overall levels of capital spending, which he then allocates across business units based not only on their list of desirable projects, but also on the strategic mission of that business.

Several years ago, we realized that our capital budgeting process was tactical in scope, and did not relate well to our company's strategic planning process. At that time, capital budgeting involved a series of quantitative procedures aimed at (a) listing individual pieces of equipment, and (b) eventually justifying their purchase through a series of small appropriation requests submitted to corporate headquarters. Apparently, our major objective was to assure that worn-out equipment would be replaced on a timely basis.

This approach to capital budgeting is beneficial in that it enables corporate management to focus on the strategic issue of the overall investment required in a given business. The planning process develops precise amounts of capital required over the near term as well as an estimate covering a longer period of time. By addressing potential manufacturing investments in this manner, we hope to avoid the risk of inadvertently increasing our investment in a particular business through small annual increments.

Notes

Chapter 1: What We Know about Capital Budgeting

1. Irving Fisher, *The Theory of Interest* (New York: Macmillan, 1930).

2. Joel Dean, *Capital Budgeting* (New York: Columbia University Press, 1951).

3. Friedrich Lutz and Vera Lutz, *The Theory of Investment of the Firm* (Princeton, N.J.: Princeton University Press, 1951).

4. Joel Dean, "Measuring the Productivity of Capital," *Harvard Business Review* (January-February 1954): 120–30.

5. J.H. Lorie and L.J. Savage, "Three Problems in Rationing Capital," *Journal of Business* (October 1955): 229–39.

6. E. Solomon, *The Management of Corporate Capital* (Glencoe, Ill.: The Free Press, 1959).

7. J. Hirshleifer, "On the Theory of Optimal Investment Decisions," *Journal of Political Economics* (August 1958): 329–52.

8. Harold Bierman and S. Smidt, *The Capital Budgeting Decision* (New York: Macmillan, 1960; 7th edi., 1988).

9. A.A. Robichek and J.G. McDonald, *Financial Management in Transition* (Menlo Park, Calif.: Stanford Research Institute, 1966), p. 7.

10. L.D. Schall, G.L. Sundem, and W.R. Geijsbeek, Jr., "Survey and Analysis of Capital Budgeting Methods," *Journal of Finance* (March 1978): 281–87.

11. D.F. Istvan, *Capital-Expenditure Decisions: How They Are Made in Large Corporations* (Bloomington: Bureau of Business Research, Indiana University, 1961), and "The Economic Evaluation of Capital Expenditures," *Journal of Business* (January 1961): 45–51.

12. Robichek and McDonald, *Financial Management in Transition.*

13. G.A. Christy, "Capital Budgeting: Current Practices and Their Efficiency," Bureau of Business and Economic Research, University of Oregon, Eugene, 1966.

14. R.B. Williams, Jr., "Industry Practice in Allocating Capital Resources," *Managerial Planning* (May-June 1970): 15–22.

15. T. Klammer, "Empirical Evidence of the Adoption of Sophisticated Capital Budgeting Techniques," *Journal of Business* (July 1972): 387–97.

16. M. Fremgen, "Capital Budgeting Practices: A Survey," *Management Accounting* (May 1973): 19–25.

17. J.W. Petty, D.F. Scott, Jr., and M.M. Bird, "The Capital Expenditure Decision-Making Process of Large Corporations," *Engineering Economist* (Spring 1975): 159–72.

18. J.W. Petty and O.D. Bowlin, "The Financial Manager and Quantitative Decision Models," *Financial Management* (Winter 1976): 32–41.

19. L.J. Gitman and J.R. Forrester, Jr., "A Survey of Capital Budgeting Techniques Used by Major U.S. Firms," *Financial Management* (Fall 1977): 66–71.

20. Schall, Sundem, and Geijsbeek, Jr., "Capital Budgeting Methods."

21. S.H. Kim, "Capital Budgeting Practices in Large Corporations and Their Impact on Overall Profitability," *Baylor Business Studies* (November-December 1978): 48–66.

22. D.J. Oblak and R.J. Helm, "Survey and Analysis of Capital Budgeting Methods Used by Multinationals," *Financial Management* (Winter 1980): 37–41.

23. S.H. Kim and E.J. Farragher, "Current Capital Budgeting Practices," *Management Accounting* (June 1981): 26–30.

24. J.S. Moore and A.K. Reichert, "An Analysis of the Financial Management Techniques Currently Employed by Large U.S. Corporations," *Journal of Business Finance and Accounting* (Winter 1983): 623–45.

25. D.F. Scott, Jr., and J.W. Petty, II, "Capital Budgeting Practices in Large American Firms: A Retrospective Analysis and Synthesis," *The Financial Review* (March 1984): 111–23.

26. M.T. Stanley and S.B. Block, "A Survey of Multinational Capital Budgeting," *The Financial Review* (March 1984): 36–51.

27. Bierman and Smidt, *The Capital Budgeting Decision,* 263–80.

28. *Financial Management,* the *Engineering Economist,* and the *Journal of Business Finance and Accounting* carry a large number of relatively readable papers on capital budgeting. The *Journal of Finance* does also, but the papers are somewhat less readable.

29. P.W. Bacon, "The Evaluation of Mutually Exclusive Investments," *Financial Management* (Summer 1977): 55–58.

30. W.L. Beedles, "A Note on Evaluating Non-Simple Investments," *Journal of Financial and Quantitative Analysis* (March 1978): 173–76.

31. R.H. Bernhard, "Mathematical Programming Models for Capital Budgeting—A Survey, Generalization, and Critique," *Journal of Financial and Quantitative Analysis* (June 1969): 111–58.

32. E.F. Brigham and R.H. Pettway, "Capital Budgeting by Utilities," *Financial Management* (Autumn 1973): 11–22.

33. E.E. Carter, "Designing the Capital Budgeting Process," *TIMS Studies in Management Science* (1977): 25–42.

34. A.V. Corr, "Capital Investment Planning," *Financial Executive* (April 1982): 12–15.

35. R. Dorfman, "The Meaning of the Internal Rate of Return," *Journal of Finance* (December 1981): 1010–23.

36. H.R. Fogler, "Ranking Techniques and Capital Rationing," *Accounting Review* (January 1972): 134–43.

37. C.G. Hoskins and G.A. Mumey, "Payback: A Maligned Method of Asset Ranking?" *Engineering Economist* (Fall 1979): 53–65.

38. S.M. Keane, "The Internal Rate of Return and the Reinvestment Fallacy," *Journal of Accounting and Business Studies* (June 1979): 48–55.

39. W.G. Lewellen, H.P. Lanser, and J.J. McConnell, "Payback Substitutes for Discounted Cash Flow," *Financial Management* (Summer 1973): 17–25.

40. J.C.T. Mao, "Survey of Capital Budgeting: Theory and Practice," *Journal of Finance* (May 1970): 349–60.

41. A. Rappaport and R.A. Taggart, Jr., "Evaluation of Capital Expenditure Proposals under Inflation," *Financial Management* (Spring 1982): 5–13.

42. M. Sarnat and H. Levy, " The Relationship of Rules of Thumb to the Internal Rate of Return: A Restatement and Generalization," *Journal of Finance* (June 1969): 479–89.

43. B. Schwab and P. Lusztig, "A Comparative Analysis of the Net Present Value and Benefit-Cost Ratios as Measures of the Economic Desirability of Investments," *Journal of Finance* (June 1969): 507–16.

44. J.B. Weaver, "Organizing and Maintaining a Capital Expenditure Program," *Engineering Economist* (Fall 1974): 1–36.

45. H.M. Weingartner, "Capital Budgeting of Interrelated Projects: Survey and Synthesis," *Management Science* (March 1966): 485–516, and "Some New Views on the Payback Period and Capital Budgeting Decisions," *Management Science* (August 1969): 594–607.

46. S.H. Archer and C.A. D'Ambrosio, *The Theory of Business Finance; A Book of Readings* (New York: Macmillan, 1976).

47. A.J. Boness, *Capital Budgeting* (New York: Praeger, 1972).

48. E.F. Brigham and R.E. Johnson, Issues in Managerial Finance, 2nd ed. (Hinsdale, Ill.: Dryden, 1980).

49. R.L. Crum and F.G.J. Derkinderen, *Capital Budgeting Under Conditions of Uncertainty* (Boston: Martinus Nijhoff, 1981).

50. L.A. Gordon and G.E. Pinches, *Improving Capital Budgeting: A Decision Support System Approach* (Reading, Mass.: Addison-Wesley, 1984).

51. E.L. Grant, W.G. Ireson, and R.S. Leavenworth, *Principles of Engineering Economy*, 6th ed. (New York: Ronald Press, 1976).

52. M. Kaufman, *The Capital Budgeting Handbook* (Homewood, Ill.: Irwin, 1986).

53. H. Levy and M. Sarnat, *Capital Investment and Financial Decisions*, 2nd ed. (Englewood Cliffs, N.J.: Prentice-Hall, 1983).

54. R.C. Lind, *Discounting for Time and Risk in Energy Policy* (Baltimore: Johns Hopkins, 1982).

55. P. Masse, *Optimal Investment Decisions: Rules for Action and Criteria for Choices* (Englewood Cliffs, N.J.: Prentice-Hall, 1962).

56. A.J. Merrett and A. Sykes, *The Finance and Analysis of Capital Projects* (New York: Wiley, 1963), and *Capital Budgeting and Company Finance* (London: Longmans, 1966).

57. G.D. Quirin and J.C. Wiginton, *Analyzing Capital Expenditures* (Homewood, Ill.: Irwin, 1981).

58. F.M. Wilkes, *Capital Budgeting Techniques* (London: Wiley, 1977).

Chapter 2: Capital Budgeting and Risk

1. See p. 68 of L.J. Gitman and J.R. Forrester, Jr., "A Survey of Capital Budgeting Techniques Used by Major U.S. Firms," *Financial Management* (Fall 1977): 66–71.

2. D.B. Hertz, "Risk Analysis in Capital Investment," *Harvard Business Review* (January-February 1964): 95–106.

3. Page 25 of E.F. Brigham, "Hurdle Rates for Screening Capital Expenditure Proposals," *Financial Management* (Autumn 1975): 17–26.

4. Page 35 of J.W. Petty and O.D. Bowlin, "The Financial Manager and Quantitative Decision Models," *Financial Management* (Winter 1976): 32–41.

5. Page 27 of L.J. Gitman and V.A. Mercurio, "Cost of Capital Techniques Used by Major U.S. Firms: Survey and Analysis of Fortune's 1,000," *Financial Management* (Winter 1982): 21–29.

6. Page 283 of L.D. Schall, G.L. Sundem, and W.R. Geijsbeek, Jr., "Survey and Analysis of Capital Budgeting Methods," *Journal of Finance* (March 1978): 281–87.

7. Brigham, "Hurdle Rates for Screening Capital Expenditure Proposals," p. 25.

8. R.S. Bower and J.M. Jenks, "Divisional Screening Rates," *Financial Management* (Autumn 1975): 42–49.

9. R.A. Taggart, Jr., "Capital Budgeting and the Financing Decision: An Exposition," *Financial Management* (Summer 1977): 59–64.

10. S.C. Myers, "Interactions of Corporate Financing and Investment Decisions—Implications for Capital Budgeting," *Journal of Finance* (March 1974): 1–25.

11. H. Hong and A. Rappaport, "Debt Capacity, Optimal Capital Structure, and Capital Budgeting Analysis," *Financial Management* (Autumn 1978): 7–11.

12. L.G. Epstein and S.M. Turnbull, "Capital Asset Prices and the Temporal Resolution of Uncertainty," *Journal of Finance* (June 1980): 627–43.

13. D.W. Mullins, "Does the Capital Asset Pricing Model Work?" *Harvard Business Review* (January-February 1982): 105-14.

14. J.F. Weston, "Investment Decisions Using the Capital Asset Pricing Model," *Financial Management* (Spring 1973): 25-33.

15. Ibid., p. 25.

16. Petty and Bowlin, "The Financial Manager and Quantitative Decision Models," p. 35.

17. Gitman and Mercurio, "Cost of Capital Techniques Used by Major U.S. Firms," p. 27.

18. S.C. Myers and S.W. Turnbull, "Capital Budgeting and the Capital Asset Pricing Model: Good News and Bad News," *Journal of Finance* (May 1977): 321-32.

19. E.F. Fama, "Risk Adjusted Discount Rates and Capital Budgeting under Certainty," *Journal of Financial Economics* (August 1977): 1-24.

20. R.J. Rendleman, Jr., "Ranking Errors in CAPM Capital Budgeting Applications," *Financial Management* (Winter 1978): 40-44.

21. H. Bierman and J.E. Hass, "Capital Budgeting under Uncertainty: A Reformulation," *Journal of Finance* (March 1973): 119-29.

22. R.S. Bower and D.R. Lessard, "An Operational Approach to Risk-Screening," *Journal of Finance* (May 1973): 321-37.

23. W.J. Breen and E.M. Lerner, "On the Use of β in Regulatory Proceedings," *Bell Journal of Economics and Management Science* (Autumn 1972): 612-21.

24. M.J. Gordon and P.J. Halpern, "Cost of Capital for a Division of a Firm," *Journal of Finance* (September 1974): 1153-63.

25. R.L. Greenfield, M.R. Randall, and J.C. Woods, "Financial Leverage and the Use of the Net Present Value Investment Criterion," *Financial Management* (Autumn 1983): 20-44).

26. D.B. Hertz, "Investment Policies That Pay Off," *Harvard Business Review* (January-February 1968): 96-108.

27. F.S. Hillier, *The Evaluation of Risky Interrelated Investments* (Amsterdam: North Holland, 1969).

28. I. Kabus, "You Can Bank on Uncertainty," *Harvard Business Review* (May-June 1976): 95-105.

29. G.D. Kesling, "Project Analysis by Computer Simulation," *Journal of System Management* (March 1970): 14-19.

30. J. Lintner, "The Valuation of Risk Assets and the Selection of Risky Investments in Stock Portfolios and Capital Budgets," *Review of Economics and Statistics* (February 1965): 13-27.

31. J.F. Magee, "How to Use Decision Trees in Capital Investment," *Harvard Business Review* (September-October 1964): 79-96.

32. E.W. Miller, "Uncertainty Induced Bias in Capital Budgeting," *Financial Management* (Autumn 1978): 12-18.

33. J.S. Moore and A.K. Reichert, "An Analysis of the Financial Management Techniques Currently Employed by Large Corporations," *Journal of Busines Finance and Accounting* (Winter 1983): 623-45.

34. M.E. Rubinstein, "A Synthesis of Corporate Financial Theory," *Journal of Finance* (March 1973): 167-81.

35. W.F. Sharpe, "Capital Asset Prices: A Theory of Market Equilibrium under Conditions of Risk," *Journal of Finance* (September 1964): 425-42.

36. W.F. Sharpe and G.M. Cooper, "Risk-Return Classes of New York Stock Exchange Common Stocks, 1931-1967," *Financial Analysts Journal* (March-April 1972): 45-54, 81, 95-101.

37. E. Solomon, "Measuring a Company's Cost of Capital," *Journal of Business* (October 1955): 95-117.

38. J.C. Van Horne, "An Application of the Capital Asset Pricing Model to Divisional Required Returns," *Financial Management* (Spring 1980): 14-19.

39. R.F. Wippern, "A Note on the Equivalent Risk Class Assumption," *Engineering Economist* (Spring 1966): 13-22.

Chapter 3: Estimating Cash Flows for Investment Analysis

1. Page 923 in C.R. Nelson, "Inflation and Capital Budgeting," *Journal of Finance* (June 1976): 923–31.

2. M.K. Kim, "Inflationary Effects in the Capital Investment Process: An Empirical Examination," *Journal of Finance* (September 1979): 941–50.

3. Page 13 in A. Rappaport and R.A. Taggart, "Evaluation of Capital Expenditure Proposals under Inflation," *Financial Management* (Spring 1982): 5–13.

4. P.L. Cooley, R.L. Roenfeldt, and I. Chew, "Capital Budgeting Procedures under Inflation," *Financial Management* (Winter 1975): 18–25.

5. A.D. Bailey, Jr., and D.L. Jensen, "General Price Level Adjustments in the Capital Budgeting Decisions," *Financial Management* (Spring 1977): 26–31.

6. Page 48 in D.R. Mehta, M.D. Curley, and H.G. Fung, "Inflation, Cost of Capital, and Capital Budgeting Procedures," *Financial Management* (Winter 1984): 48–54.

7. A. Gandolfi, "Inflation, Taxes and Interest Rates," *Journal of Finance* (June 1982): 797–807.

8. J.R. Ezzell and W.A. Kelly, Jr., "An APV Analysis of Capital Budgeting under Inflation," *Financial Management* (Autumn 1984): 49–54.

9. P.L. Cooley, R.L. Roenfeldt, and I. Chew, "Capital Budgeting Procedures under Inflation," *Financial Management* (Autumn 1976): 87–90.

10. M.C. Findlay, III, "Capital Budgeting Procedures under Inflation," *Financial Management* (Autumn 1976): 83–86.

11. A.W. Frankle, "Capital Budgeting Procedures under Inflation," *Financial Management* (Autumn 1976): 86–87.

12. J.S. Schell and R.S. Nicolosi, "Capital Expenditure Feedback: Project Reappraisal," *Engineering Economist* (Summer 1974): 253–61.

13. J.C. Van Horne, "A Note on Biases in Capital Budgeting Introduced by Inflation," *Journal of Financial and Quantitative Analysis* (March 1971): 653–58.

Chapter 4: Capital Budgeting and Capital Rationing

1. Page 1404 in H.M. Weingartner, "Capital Rationing: *n* Authors in Search of a Plot," *Journal of Finance* (December 1977): 1403–31.

2. H.M. Weingartner, *Mathematical Programming and the Analysis of Capital Budgeting Problems* (Englewood Cliffs, N.J.: Prentice-Hall, 1963).

3. W. Baumol and R. Quandt, "Investment and Discount Rates under Capital Rationing—A Programming Approach," *Economic Journal* (June 1965): 317–29.

4. Page 55 in P.W. Bacon, "The Evaluation of Mutually Exclusive Investments," *Financial Management* (Summer 1977): 55–58.

5. Weingartner, "Capital Rationing," p. 1430.

6. Ibid.

7. Page 130 in H.E. Thompson, "Mathematical Programming, The Capital Asset Pricing Model and Capital Budgeting of Inter-related Projects," *Journal of Finance* (March 1976): 125–31.

8. Page 19 in D.F. Rychel, "Capital Budgeting with Mixed Integer Linear Programming: An Application," *Financial Management* (Winter 1977) 11–19.

9. R.H. Bernhard, "Mathematical Programming Models for Capital Budgeting—A Survey, Generalization, and Critique," *Journal of Financial and Quantitative Analysis* (June 1969): 111–58.

10. R.M. Burton, and W.W. Damon, "On the Existence of a Cost of Capital under Pure Capital Rationing," *Journal of Finance* (September 1974): 1165–74.

11. W.T. Carleton, "Linear Programming and Capital Budgeting Models: A New Interpretation," *Journal of Finance* (December 1969): 825–33.

12. E.J. Elton, "Capital Rationing and External Discount Rates," *Journal of Finance* (June 1970): 573–84.

13. J.D. Forsyth and D.C. Owen, "Capital Rationing Methods," in R.L. Crum and F.G.J. Derkinderen, eds. *Capital Budgeting under Conditions of Uncertainty* (Boston: Martinus Nijhoff, 1981): 213–35.

14. J. Hirshleifer, "On the Theory of Optimal Investment," *Journal of Political Economy* (August 1958): 329–52.

15. J.H. Lorie and L.J. Savage, "Three Problems in Rationing Capital," *Journal of Business* (October 1955): 229–39.

16. P. Lusztig and B. Schwab, "A Note on the Application of Linear Programming to Capital Budgeting," *Journal of Financial and Quantitative Analysis* (December 1968): 427–31.

17. A.S. Manne, "Optimal Dividend and Investment Policies for a Self-Financing Business Enterprise," *Management Science* (November 1968): 119–29.

18. L.J. Merville and L.A. Tavis, "A Generalized Model for Capital Investment," *Journal of Finance* (March 1973): 109–18.

19. S.C. Myers, "A Note on Linear Programming and Capital Budgeting," *Journal of Finance* (March 1972): 89–92.

20. S.C. Myers and G.A. Pogue, "A Programming Approach to Corporate Financial Management," *Journal of Finance* (May 1974): 579–99.

21. G.A. Whitmore and L.R. Amey, "Capital Budgeting under Rationing: Comments on the Lusztig and Schwab Procedure," *Journal of Financial and Quantitative Analysis* (January 1973): 127–35.

Chapter 5: Capital Budgeting and Corporate Strategy

1. W.T. Carleton, "An Analytical Model for Long-Range Financial Planning," *Journal of Finance* (May 1970): 291–315.

2. J.W. Elliot, "Forecasting and Analysis of Corporate Financial Performance with an Econometric Model of the Firm," *Journal of Financial and Quantitative Analysis* (March 1972): 1499–1526.

3. J.C. Francis and D.R. Rowell, "A Simultaneous Equation Model of the Firm for Financial Analysis and Planning," *Financial Management* (Spring 1978): 29–44.

4. G.W. Gershefski, "Building a Corporate Financial Model," *Harvard Business Review* (July-August 1969): 61–72.

5. S.C. Myers and G.A. Pogue, "A Programming Approach to Corporate Financial Management," *Journal of Finance* (May 1974): 579–99.

6. J.M. Warren and J.P. Shelton, "A Simultaneous Equation Approach to Financial Planning," *Journal of Finance* (December 1971): 1123–42.

7. H.M. Weingartner, *Mathematical Programming and the Analysis of Capital Budgeting Problems* (Chicago: Markham Publishing, 1967).

8. H.M. Weingartner, "Some New Views on the Payback Period and Capital Budgeting Decisions," *Management Science*, Application series (August 1969): B-594–B-601.

9. Page 92 in H.R. Fogler, "Overkill in Capital Budgeting Technique?" *Financial Management* (Spring 1972): 92–96.

10. Page 36 in K.L. Hastie, "One Businessman's View of Capital Budgeting," *Financial Management* (Winter 1974): 36–44.

11. Ibid.

12. Page 6 in G.E. Pinches, "Myopia, Capital Budgeting and Decision Making," *Financial Management* (Autumn 1982): 6–19.

13. H. Bierman, Jr., "Strategic Capital Budgeting," *Financial Executive* (April 1979): 22–24.

14. M.E. Porter, *Competitive Strategy* (New York: The Free Press, 1980).

15. S. Mason and R.C. Merton, "The Role of Contingent Claims Analysis in Corporate Finance," in *Recent Advances in Corporate Finance* E. Altman and M. Subrahmanyam, eds., (Homewood, Ill.: Irwin, 1985).

16. L. Trigeorgis and S.P. Mason, "Valuing Managerial Flexibility," *Midland Corporate Finance Journal* (Spring 1987): 14–21.

17. F. Black and M. Scholes, "The Pricing of Options and Corporate Liabilities," *Journal of Political Economy* 3 (1973): 637–59.

Index

About the Author

Harold Bierman, Jr. is the Nicholas H. Noyes Professor of Business Administration at Cornell University. A Cornell faculty member since 1956, Professor Bierman has taught accounting, financial policy, and investments. He formerly was on the faculties at Louisiana State University, the University of Michigan, and the University of Chicago. He is a recent recipient of the Dow Jones Award from the American Assembly of Collegiate Schools of Business for his outstanding contributions to collegiate business education. In 1985 he served as scholar-in-residence at Prudential Bache. His industrial experience includes work with Corning Glass Works, Arthur Young and Company, Shell Oil Company, Ford Motor Company, and Xerox Corporation. He has written numerous books, including *The Capital Budgeting Decision* (with Seymour Smidt), *Financial Accounting, Managerial Accounting*, and *Financial Policy Decisions*, and over a hundred journal articles.

Implementing Capital Budgeting Techniques

Revised Edition
A Financial Management Association Book
The Institutional Investor Series in Finance

Harold Bierman, Jr.

Over thirty years have elapsed since new techniques were developed to improve capital budgeting decisions. But no current book has taken stock of the many difficulties financial managers encounter in trying to assess their long-term investment. Regardless of the method they use for evaluating competing projects, they're sure to discover that the investment decision can never be solved by a single mathematical technique. Instead, the capital budget decision must be implemented within the strategic plan and operating budget of the firm. This is the central challenge facing financial managers when planning their long-term capital outlays.

Harold Bierman, Jr., understands this challenge. He surveyed 257 financial officers from the largest Fortune 500 industrial firms, asking them to identify the barriers they encounter in implementing capital budgeting techniques. The wealth of replies he received forms the empirical foundation for **Implementing Capital Budgeting Techniques.**
Bierman thoroughly examines the problems as perceived by these financial managers, including risk, integrating the budgeting with the overall business strategy, determining the hurdle rate, and communicating the rationale for the budgeting process. He succeeds in linking the academic literature to the current interests of business managers, providing them with a framework for coping with their difficulties.

For corporate finance officers and business managers who want to improve their ability to make capital investment decisions, and for scholars of corporate finance and financial management, **Implementing Capital Budgeting Techniques** describes methods for implementing known capital budgeting techniques that can be used with confidence. Equally important, it conveys a realistic understanding of the *limits* of academic knowledge concerning capital budgeting.

Harold Bierman, Jr., is the Nicholas H. Noyes Professor of Business Administration at Cornell University. A Cornell faculty member since 1956, Professor Bierman formerly taught accounting, financial policy, and investment at Louisiana State University, the University of Michigan, and the University of Chicago. He is a recent recipient of the Dow Jones Award from the American Assembly of Collegiate Schools of Business for his contribution to collegiate business education. In 1985 he served as scholar-in-residence at Prudential Bache. His industrial experience includes work with Corning Glass Works, Shell Oil Company, Ford Motor Company, and Xerox Corporation. He has written numerous books, including *The Capital Budgeting Decision* (with Seymour Smidt), *Financial Accounting, Managerial Accounting,* and *Financial Policy Decisions,* and over a hundred journal articles.